Chattanooga
C H R O N I C L E S

Chattanooga
CHRONICLES

Cody Maxwell

Charleston · London

THE
History
PRESS

Published by The History Press
Charleston, SC 29403
www.historypress.net

Cover images: Painting on front courtesy of the Library of Congress, Prints and Photographs Division. Photo on back of Chief John Ross Bridge by Carol M. Highsmith, courtesy of the Carol M. Highsmith Archive, Library of Congress, Prints and Photographs Division.

First published 2013

Manufactured in the United States

ISBN 978.1.60949.658.6

Library of Congress CIP data applied for.

*For Brother Simon,
and with gratitude to* The Pulse *and to Janis Hashe.*

CONTENTS

PREFACE

L ooking back into its history, Chattanooga was no different than any other southern city. It had its slaves and its lynchings over the river. It killed the Indians. Its rich were fat and its poor starved. The Klan did what they did in Chattanooga just like they did in Mississippi and Alabama. Chattanooga was the same as any other southern town.

But that big government up north put a stop to most of that long ago, and Chattanooga moved on. It grew from a swampy mud hole by the river to a real river and railroad town, a small city that was on the verge of becoming the most powerful city in the South. This Chattanooga—the "Dynamo of Dixie," the city was called—was built on the backs of steelworkers. Steel foundries and river commerce built this city. Heavy work and working men raised the town. This factory town continued to grow until, not very long ago and despite all that hard work, Chattanooga was known as the most polluted, filthy city in the entire country. Walter Cronkite, the most trusted man in the news business, told the world so on his nightly television show. Foundries and steel mills spit out their smoke and fumes, and that ugly smog hung heavy in the air. It was gray in the daytime then, and the air stank. The Walnut Street Bridge was still just an old bridge, and Coolidge Park was an overgrown field where dope fiends and the homeless camped out. North Chattanooga was still "Hill City," the ghetto spot across the river that white folks steered clear of. There was no fresh-water aquarium. There were no ice cream shops or playgrounds. There were smoking foundries that were the lifeblood of the city, and there was, in the opinions of many, a slum city on the side of the river with oily smokestacks and a couple of fish head restaurants.

But times do change. Times change every day, and Chattanooga is not that old river town anymore. The city has undergone a remarkable face-lift in the past thirty years. It's had a succession of mayors who have done the remarkable job of transforming it into the urban playground that it has become. Chattanooga is no longer a steel foundry and river town—the city is now driven by the hospitality industry. From Main Street to the Riverfront, downtown has become the pride and joy of the city's more affluent residents and a destination point for tourists. Major hotels are everywhere, and the convention center brings thousands upon thousands of visitors to the city every year. There are 3D theaters and water fountains for the visiting children to splash in. There are music festivals and a great big aquarium, art museums and beer festivals. There's some sort of publically funded metal sculpture on every corner, for better or for worse and until such things go the way of shag carpet. There are ecofriendly electric buses circling Market and Broad Streets. A new restaurant seems to open on some downtown street corner every few months, and Track 29 has finally filled that hole that everybody says the yearly Riverbend Festival leaves behind—the want of relevant musical acts. There are a couple of gay bars around a couple of corners and ethnic parades through the center of town every now and then. The Twelve Tribes, a self-ostracizing religious group who run a restaurant near the college, have returned after thirty years in exile. They were run out of town back in the '70s, but they've been allowed to return home, and no one has bothered them. There are godly churches galore—from Muslim to Jewish to Billy Graham Baptist—and they never bother the atheists who sit around and blaspheme openly in the hip coffee shops around town. Clay Bennett, the brilliant, universally applauded political cartoonist, was even given a job by the *Chattanooga Times Free Press*. He leans slightly toward the political left, causing some of the old-timers to refer to him as that "Commie bastard," but the young people look up to him. He has made the city proud. What more moral or economic reconstruction could be asked of an old southern town?

Summer tourists come here to ride "America's Most Amazing Mile" and visit dead Confederate battlefields. They go to Point Park to see the cold cannons and that big panorama up there. They ride the Incline back down the mountain and sleep in

Welders at a Chattanooga Steel Plant. *Library of Congress.*

quaint old rail cars at the Chattanooga Choo-Choo—the waitresses there sing to them while they eat cheese and chicken. They go shopping along Frazier Avenue, then visit the boutiques and all the art galleries and museums in the Bluff View Art District. They drink espressos and eat Danishes at Rembrandt's. They go to the symphony and opera on Friday evenings or to riverfront concerts in the summer and have dinner at Chato afterward. The steel foundry work bells don't ring around Chattanooga anymore, and the races mostly leave one another alone. Despite its smoggy and bigoted past, Chattanooga has become one of America's most attractive cities and one of the finest places a person can call home. Its beauty is unsurpassed—its mountains and its river are the envy of every other mid-sized city around. The people are wonderful, and the entire world has taken notice—that mayoral face-lift was remarkably successful. Chattanooga has become bright and vibrant to outside eyes.

There is something beneath it all, though, and to those native to the city, all is a shade darker. There is something there—something undeniably strange about the town. Those who have been here long enough know it, but nobody can pinpoint precisely what it is. There is a spirit here that is both shameful and comfortable, something that is publicly denied but privately cherished. It doesn't have a name—it's not something that can be tied down with a string of words. It's something else. There are a few from Chattanooga who just blindly accept whatever it is and simply call it home.

Others, in a somewhat similar way, laughingly call the city a black hole. If you are from Chattanooga, you can leave, they say. You can leave for extended periods of time, even. But you'll be back. Something always brings you back. These natives laugh about this over rattling glass, hip music and Pabst Blue

Civil War cannon and the city panorama atop Lookout Mountain. *Author's collection.*

The Chattanooga Incline Railway. *Author's collection.*

Ribbon at the Pickle Barrel. They especially laugh as they wave goodbye to hometown friends who have decided to move on to better places such as Colorado, New York or San Francisco. These natives laugh at their naïve and wayward friends as they pull away from some North Chattanooga or St. Elmo side street, heading for the highway. These naïve friends get laughed at again and have a chair pulled out for them when, a few months or maybe a year later, the Pickle Barrel's heavy door closes behind them, and they walk back into that cloud of cigarette smoke and music. The bartender, Avery—the best bartender in Chattanooga, by the way—always remembers what they drink. He slides them a cold one, and they're back home again, road-worn, a little wiser and sitting elbow to elbow with the same old people in the same old town they swore they would never see again.

We are all tied to the soil, whether we like it or not. Every soul on earth is. It's a strange aspect of humanity. Perhaps not as closely tied to the dirt as we were when the earth had to be worked with our hands in order to eat and stay alive, but even now, in the age of drive-thru joints and Walmarts, we're still tied to the place we call home. A person can reflect on, diarize and psychoanalyze their lives all they want to, but they'll never truly understand who they are, what makes them strong and good or what makes them twisted and wrong unless they seek to know the people and the land they came from.

While certainly not a ghost town (there are no tumbleweeds blowing through its streets), Chattanooga is certainly a town full of dead people and ghosts. They froth up all the time. Some of these old haints are celebrated: the sacrifices of those Confederate boys lying dead on the battlefields that cover the city like a skin disease, the moneymaking nostalgia that is the Chattanooga Choo-Choo and even that old dead prostitute in room 311 at the Read House—all these and more are held near and dear to the heart of Chattanooga. It's all become eerily romantic and nostalgic. Everybody knows those stories. But there are other stories that have been swept away or have been exorcised by those who have written the city's history. These old specters have not disappeared but hide, confined to forgotten cemeteries, the dusty pages of unread books, the hollow caves in the mountains and the tunnels beneath the city streets. They are the fearful ones—the true ghosts. They're the ones this book has tried to capture. They are who hold the secret.

My boy, Simon, asked me one time why I write books. Why do you spend all day Saturday at the library when you keep saying that you need to mow the grass? Why don't you just mow the grass, so we can go fishing like you said? I told him it was because I had a deadline—I promised someone a few stories and had to have them done at a certain time—but that wasn't the truth. The truth is that we are all going to die. We are all going to be dust under some gray tombstone someday. Whether it's in the old Citizens Cemetery or in Forest Hills Cemetery at the foot of Lookout Mountain, beneath the ground is where we're all going to be. We are all heading to the same place. And in telling the stories of a few old ordinaries from the past, I hope to leave something of a portrait of who we all were.

I am also one of the many who have tried to leave this place. I laughed when the others laughed and said they would see me again soon, but I swore I would not be back. There's nothing here, I said, and no reason for me to hang around Chattanooga. I'm not into the hospitality industry, and it's a dead-end town, I said.

But here I am, in an all-night diner on McCallie Avenue with a book full of Chattanooga stories on my lap, attempting to understand this thing called home. I'm certainly not ashamed to be here, but I would like to know why I still am. Maybe I'll figure it all out soon, and my work here will save my boy the trouble of figuring it all out on his own someday.

Though I've written a number of historical tales, don't expect this to be your standard history book. I have not tried to offer a concise and complete history of anything. I have merely flipped through the photo album of Chattanooga's past to see what this city is and who we really are. My boy and I have dug behind dumpsters and along the banks of old creeks that run under bridges where the hoboes still live, through overgrown cemeteries, inside smoky railroad tunnels and through typewritten manuscripts that nobody cares about, not to write yet another chapter on Chattanooga's involvement in the Civil War, but to find out who we are. The great democracy that we are declares that "We, the People" are of much more importance than any old war, anyway. What matters to us are the daily struggles and accomplishments of people like us—those from our town, our own "half acre of paradise." They had our habits and our beliefs and disbeliefs, and even though they are all gone now, they matter more than men who led other men to their deaths. Those old soldiers and war generals have historical markers and monuments all over the city—we have none. I hope that this book will stand as something resembling one.

One last note—quickly and while I have you here: I must admit a huge debt of gratitude to the Twelve Tribes, the folks who have the restaurant called the Yellow Deli near the college downtown. This may be inappropriate, and I'm no member of their family—I don't even know any of their names—but they let me set myself up with piles of books, old newspapers, overflowing manila folders and my laptop, all spread across their tables, and they always leave me undisturbed for hours on end. I buy an occasional sandwich or slice of banana bread from them, but my rent has never really been paid. I know I've overstayed my welcome. I've drunk gallons of their sweet tea and wrote a great bit of these words while sitting in their house. And when I occasionally grew tired of all this and wanted to forget about it all for a while, I dozed off on their old leather couches, listening to the music they play, and I was always left unbothered.

I don't understand them, but I thank them.

THE OLD ORCHARD KNOB

Andy Williams was his name. Chattanooga's story may not have begun with him, but he was here when Chattanooga's story began. Andy moved here with his father when he was still a little boy. The Williams family was among the first white men to call this land along the river home. They moved here long before it was Chattanooga—when it was an untamed wilderness still owned by the Indians. The Tennessee River ran wild in those days.

There was nothing special about Andy. He never grew into a brave Civil War soldier or a great statesman. Andy was never mayor of the city. He was not even a sheriff. He is not remembered for anything particularly heroic or for any innovative, cotton gin–like inventions. There has been no place carved for him in the hallowed halls of proper history. No one painted his portrait—we can only imagine what he might have looked like. His life was surely one of childish play when he was young and of work and sleep once he became a man, as most of our lives are. Andy Williams means as much to academic history as any other body lying beneath some faded old Chattanooga tombstone. He's just a pile of dust or bones in a black hole somewhere now. He lived in Chattanooga for a little while. He played in the woods when he was a boy and grew a garden when he became a man. He walked Chattanooga's old green hills and fished in its river and creeks. He married a girl and raised a few children. He lived his life. He lived his life rather simply, and he was lucky enough to have died an old man one day. He was no different than any of us.

Why we know anything at all about Andy Williams now is because of a few letters he wrote to a man named Henry Wiltse. This man Wiltse wrote a historical column for an old Chattanooga newspaper. Andy was an elderly man by the time Henry Wiltse came along, and Henry would often contact him for stories about Chattanooga's earliest years. Andy knew those times and remembered them very well. Parts of his letters from Andy Williams and other historical notes by Mr. Wiltse are kept in Chattanooga's downtown library, bound together as part of a history of the city the writer began but life didn't allow him the time to complete.

Andy was a young boy when his father floated his family down the Tennessee River and landed them at Ross's Landing. It was 1835, and there was no Chattanooga in those days. There was only Chief John Ross's landing on the riverbank. There was one white man's cabin on the south side of the river that was occupied by the ferryman; the rest was lush and expansive wilderness. Andy's father was able to secure through the government an "occupant's right" to a section of land that was then known as Bald Knob, a hilly stretch of land in a valley a few miles east of Ross's Landing. His father planted corn at the foot of Bald Knob and a fruit orchard over its sides. The corn did quite well, but it was the orchard that was most impressive and apparently quite successful, for it was from the fruitful labors of Andy's father that the old bald hill eventually became known as Orchard Knob.

His father built a cabin for the family near where Bushtown now is, and as a young boy, Andy roamed the new land around him for miles. The first thing he remembered about the land was the Indian tents, he said, which were "thicker than trees." When he played alone in the woods and fields, Andy would sometimes see the Indians passing in bands. He listened to their songs and watched the smoke rising from the fires around their teepees. When Andy was alone, he always watched the Indians from afar—he was taught not to go near them without his father and his father's gun.

The young boy chased animals through the trees and pulled fish out of the creeks. He picked blackberries and wild fruits for his mother. He saw bands of deer grazing in the fields and heard wild coyotes call. He lay on his back in the fields and among wildflowers at night listening to the whippoorwills sing and to nightingales crying their songs. The land he lay in was a wild Eden. One of Andy's letters to the historian Henry Wiltse described what the Chattanooga landscape was like in those early years:

> *The spies that Moses sent out to search the land of Canaan could not have found a more beautiful valley, with everything to sustain life either growing or running wild in the woods, except bread. Upon river and creek bottoms grew as fine timber as ever grew on earth. There was a sycamore that stood just below the fork of Citico Creek, which at the height of twenty or twenty-five feet had three prongs, and when I saw it, it had a door just large enough so a man could go through it. We cut the door large enough so a horse could go*

in, turn around and come out, and I kept dry there out of many a summer shower of rain.

Of good things to eat that grew in the bottoms were the May-apple, the hazelnut, walnut, muscadine, winter grape, wild plum and mulberry. The wild plum trees grew in clusters. The plums were not so large as some of the tame ones, but were the most delicious I ever ate. Around these hills and knobs grew the sugar, red and black haw, the summer grape, the persimmon and prickly pear. And in the black glades, wild onion by the bushel.

Of four footed beasts, there was everything from the little striped ground squirrel to the rabbit and deer. For the night hunter was the coon, the possum, and look out for the skunk. Among the squirrels, the gray squirrel was the most. We never thought of a pet squirrel. They were so plentiful that they were all pets.

Of the feathered tribe was from the little tomtit to the turkey. The wild pigeon would come in the fall after the mast, until I have seen acres covered in a flutter with them. The wild goose came from the cold north to warmer climes in droves and would often stop and winter with us. I have seen the elements darkened by the crows going to their roosts on the mountains and coming off in the morning. The buzzards would sail around in front of a summer cloud.

The next structure nearest to Andy's home was Straw Tavern, which catered to the men traveling up and down the river speculating on the virgin land and trading with the Indians. The tavern stood at what is now the corner of Vine and Willow Streets in the Orchard Knob neighborhood. It was conducted by a man named Pryor, and Andy said "Hell Hole" might have been a more appropriate name for it. There was whiskey to be had, the area's only deck of cards and a pack of loud, baying hounds that was kept out back. Occasionally, there were women. Andy was sure of at least one murder that had been committed there. The poor murder victim was buried with little ceremony among his father's trees atop the old Orchard Knob.

On occasion, Andy had to hang around the tavern waiting on his father, who had to meet a man there for some reason or other. While there, he would hear dark tales about happenings beyond his father's protection. There were strange stories that came up from farther down the river, along a stretch of turbulent water there called the Narrows, where a terrible, murderous band of outlaw Indians lived. There were tales of a cave there—a dark and evil cave that harbored the renegade Chickamauga Indians and murderous river pirates. These stories haunted the young boy's nights and added that small bit of danger that is always necessary in any young boy's reckoning of paradise.

But Andy wasn't a regular at the Straw Tavern, nor was his hardworking father. Andy was still a boy then, and his father didn't have time to tarry with the wayfarers. There was work to be done at home and in the fields. "Every toddler that could halloo and run was kept busy keeping the crows and squirrels out of the corn," Andy said, "if we were to gather any in the fall." But there was some spare time, and the boy spent most of it roaming the virgin countryside around Orchard Knob. He walked up and down the creeks that all flowed to the river, through the forests and over the hills that few white men had ever seen. There were fish in the river and creeks in such abundance that he could catch them as fast as he could throw out a hook with a long stick pole. There was magic there—in the whippoorwilling birds at night and lightning bugs that lit up the dark trees. There were dangerous, war-painted Indians lurking behind the lightning bugs and old, dark trees—Andy was sure of it.

There were even rumors of buried treasure. It became whispered around Straw Tavern and among the men in the fields one year that a man named W.D. Fulton, a bank cashier, secretly buried a large amount of money and gold somewhere around Orchard Knob. This Mr. Fulton then left the area and had not returned. The rumors of this hidden cache of money and gold brought men from near and far to dig around Andy's Orchard Knob, hoping to find the buried loot.

One such group of men found a strange and obviously unnatural indentation in the ground among the old fruit trees. These men laughed aloud and became greatly encouraged. They hooted and hollered and began digging with near frantic zest, believing that they had finally found the right spot. They dug and laughed and dug, planning how they would spend their newfound riches before they were even excavated. These treasure-seeking men were convinced that each shovel full of dirt they cast away from them was bringing them a little closer to a trouble-free life of luxury. The men dug and laughed and dug until one of their shovels struck something hard and hollow. It certainly wasn't another rock, and the men all threw their shovels aside and cried aloud. They lifted the object from the ground and excitedly brushed the dirt away. To their horror and dismay, the men soon saw that they had not unearthed their box of riches. What they held in their hands was the skull of the man who had years earlier been murdered at the Straw Tavern and buried in a grave on Orchard Knob. The men threw the skull on the ground and fearfully gave up their search for the money and gold. They all ran quickly back to their wives and hardworking lives, not even bothering to rebury the bones of the poor dead man they had unearthed.

Chattanooga grew quickly during those early days. Streets were scraped out of the mud, and storefronts grew up from the ground. Churches were raised, and God came to Chattanooga. Sheriffs and judges were put to work to create some kind of order out of the chaos of the wild land and the brazen pioneers who came to tame it. Cornfields and tobacco grew. Corn liquor was then distilled, and the tobacco was smoked in taverns that were built down by the river. Fights broke out, and men were shot sometimes. Jailhouses and courthouses were made to deal with such problems. Boys met girls and new children were born and Chattanooga continued to grow. Schoolhouses were built, educated schoolteachers were brought in to teach the children their three "R"s and the fruit trees planted by Andy's father on the sides of Orchard Knob did well.

One day, one of those new schoolteachers visited Orchard Knob. He was a young man named Sam Morris. Sam and a small band of young ladies went out for an autumn stroll one evening. In those days, schoolteachers were expected to be perpetually unwed so that their lives could be devoted entirely to the students in their care, and this Sam Morris had come to enjoy the perpetual benefits of the unmarried life. He strolled knowingly and most poetically over the hill. He delighted the young ladies who followed him with tales of the old poets and misty, faraway places. He laughed confidently, and the eyelashes of the blushing young ladies waved at him as they followed close behind.

After a while, Sam Morris and his ladies came upon a nest of whippoorwills in one of the fruit trees atop Orchard Knob. Sam gently took the small birds from their nest and placed them in the young ladies' trembling hands. The girls were enamored of the little birds—they had, of course, heard the whippoorwill's plaintive cries in the night but had most likely never held the bird that cried so beautifully under the twilight stars. Sam laughed at the swooning girls who held the delicate nightbirds in their hands, and they all continued on their stroll. Soon, they happened across the hole that had been left in the ground by the treasure-seeking men. They all speculated on why the hole in the ground may have appeared, and none of them could figure out why. The baby whippoorwills cried softly in the young ladies' hands.

Seeing something odd lying nearby, Sam knelt down and examined the object. He leaned close to the earth and picked the object up. Sam Morris then chuckled a little. The young girls leaned close over his shoulders, asking him what he had found. The young schoolteacher rose and turned to his ladies, holding forth the skull of the poor man who had been murdered at the Straw Tavern and unearthed by the treasure seekers. The ladies gasped, but the schoolteacher calmed the ladies and took the baby whippoorwills from their hands. Sam placed the delicate birds inside the dusty skull of the dead man.

He held it aloft. All the girls listened to the whippoorwills' soft cooing from inside their strange cage. Sam then strolled knowingly away with the skull and the whippoorwills in his hand as evening's gray light fell. The haunted young ladies whispered and giggled among themselves and followed even more closely behind the schoolteacher Sam Morris. They followed him over to the backside of the darkening Orchard Knob.

As the years passed, ever more white men began stepping off boats and rafts with their families at Ross's Landing. They walked into the fertile valleys and soft hills surrounding the river and made those lands their home. That small town that grew out of the fields and trees near the river became a small community. The wilds along the river became civilized, and men's hearts grew. Andy's Orchard Knob remained as his father had made it, though—that big, strange hill covered with fruit trees just to the east of town. And as the schoolteacher Sam Morris had already discovered, the old Orchard Knob was a wonderful place for lovers and sentimentally inclined young people. Though Andy had come to know the old hill while he was only a rambunctious young boy, he couldn't remain that small boy forever. Soon, always too soon, that strange hold those annoying young girls always come to take on a young man's heart did not spare Andy. One cool afternoon in a now long-forgotten November, Andy found himself among his father's fruit trees. He was not going to work, nor was he going fishing or chasing squirrels or fireflies. This was a very serious day for the boy. Of this late autumn day, Andy later wrote:

> There were a dozen or fifteen girls and boys, all in their teens, who went forth to gather the delicious fruit growing in the orchards. The girls were dressed in their homespun dresses and sunbonnets, while the boys were in their shirt sleeves, with copperas galluses and brogan shoes; but as the November sun reflected the yellow and brown leaves we scaled the rocks as lightly as the Rocky Mountain kids. I had gone to the south side and seated myself, with a fair hand in mine, the love vine twining and creeping around my heart, and for the first time in my life I realized that someone was standing between me and my mother. My ears were greeted with the exclamation—"O, run here, do, and see what I have found!" In less than two minutes there were a dozen or fifteen heads packed as close as heads could be, all eyes looking into a hollow tree. In there were four half-grown kittens, all ring-striped and spotted, with bushy tails, snugged in a nest as snug as can be, but not long to remain there. They were soon hauled off, and of course the girls had the first grab. They pressed them to their bosoms with such expressions as—"Bless your little

heart—you are mine!" But then—Oh pshaw! Great Heavens! Good Lord! I
have never scented such an odor from that day to this, and on my sweetheart
too! The kittens were little skunks!

It can only be supposed that Andy recovered from this incident with the
baby skunks. We can only hope that his sweetheart recovered, too, for this is as
far as Andy's letters to Henry Wiltse go. How he went on with the rest of his
days is unsure. Surely he married, became a father himself and held his boy's
hand and walked him over the old Orchard Knob. He must have worked,
he must have been a respectable citizen, but we really don't know. These
few small anecdotes are all there is—little bits of letters in which an old man
remembered his boyhood home. Andy died on August 14, 1913, having never
traveled too far from that old bald hill where his daddy planted an orchard.

This is admittedly not much of a story in the grand scheme of historical
lives. Andy Williams never meant for his life to be grand, though—he simply
wanted to live. But the light his letters shed on the land he grew up on gave
that land a life all its own. It's a land that people now drive their cars over
every day. They stop for stop signs and red lights on paved streets around
Orchard Knob now. They watch out for policemen and street people on the
street corners rather than for bands of Indians or birds or clouds up in the
sky. While Andy's few words may not be important to most people, they are
certainly poignant and remind us of the hope those first Chattanoogans saw
in the city's mountains, valleys and that big river.

It was ninety-nine years after Andy died, almost to the day, that I came upon
these fragments of letters in that dusty, unread library book. The last thing I
read was a bit of one other letter he'd written to Henry Wiltse. Henry had
sent him questions about the Union occupation of Orchard Knob during the
Civil War. Andy responded with his stories of General Grant and his cold
soldiers, of dead horses and cannon shots, of masses of men shot and dying
or starving. Andy had seen all these things, and he wrote what he knew to help
the inquisitive historian. But suddenly and without warning in his letter, Andy
abruptly dismissed all the war stories and other events he deemed unworthy
of remembrance and asked Henry not to ask him about the war anymore.
That war was not his life and did not figure in his memories of home. "Let
me return to my childhood days at Orchard Knob," he wrote. "It was there
at that Knob that I tugged my sled up and slid down a thousand times. It was
at this knob that I sat and listened to the bark of the squirrel, and woke up the
whippoorwills as they sailed around, and heard them make their peculiar cries
in the air. It was here that I listened to the deep basso profundo of the bullfrog,

and now and then heard the hoot of a wise old owl away down in the bottoms. It was here, under the trees, that I used to dream of years to come."

Progress stomped its heavy boots over the years that came. It brought railroads and fevers and mayors and wars. The Indians in their teepees were

Civil War monuments on Orchard Knob. *Library of Congress.*

forced out, and slaves were brought in. Trees fell and mountains were leveled and houses and storefronts grew in their place. Steamboats came hollering down the big foggy river. Bridges were built, washed out by floods and then built up again. Jails and electricity and automobiles, all these things—progress and men ever-wanting more created a new landscape and a new society that had no need of anything besides wealth and perpetual expansion.

These days, when the name Orchard Knob is mentioned, an old hill or fruit orchard is not what comes to mind. Orchard Knob is the name of the neighborhood surrounding the hill, a neighborhood often mentioned in the newspaper and on the local evening news. It's said that decent people only go there to buy things they really don't need and usually end up getting mugged, stabbed or shot.

The actual hill that was once covered in fruit trees—Chattanooga's Orchard Knob—is a monument to the Civil War now, the same war Andy Williams dismissed in his letter so that he could remember the days of his youth. General Grant had his headquarters there when Chattanooga was in the throes of that old war, and the city today doesn't want to forget it. Despite all its rich and varied history, this town has for some reason acquired a great fondness for the part it played in the war, at the expense of a place as strangely romantic as Andy's Orchard Knob. It seems a bit sad atop the old hill now, and it brings to mind that old poet who sang:

> Alas, that Spring should vanish with the Rose!
> That Youth's sweet-scented Manuscript should close!
> The Nightingale that in the Branches sang,
> Ah, whence, and whither flown again, who knows?

Where have all those old things gone? Some eastern Buddha-man once said that you can never put your hand in the same river twice. What's past is gone forever, and perhaps that's true, but if so, it would really be nice if that same brutal and fleeting time could wear down those silly monuments to dead wars and soldiers a bit faster. It's strange the things people honor. Where young girls would once promenade in their clean dresses and sunbonnets, carrying wildflowers and laughing at the boys, or where those girls went strolling with the dandy schoolteacher Sam Morris, where young Andy Williams would run through October nights to lie on his back to listen to nightingales sing and to watch the moon go by—that place, Andy's old Orchard Knob, is now littered with larger-than-life marble soldiers, overgrown grass, cannons and American flags.

THE TURKEY THEFT

G iven the debt every Chattanooga historian owes to the unfinished manuscript Henry Wiltse left behind, and that the Chattanooga Library has so finely preserved, I feel this book must show its respects to a particular tale Mr. Wiltse recorded while writing down his history of Chattanooga. As the reader will soon learn, Wiltse recorded this story out of an honorable sense of obligation to the protagonist of the tale and to preserve for the ages the simple morality the small tale holds. So, out of sincere respect for the unrecognized work of Mr. Henry Wiltse and for a certain old noble thief called Mr. Weathers, I feel equally obliged to make sure this little snippet of Chattanooga history is preserved and shared.

I considered rewriting this tale and phrasing it in a more modern language, but reading the story with this idea in mind, it quickly became obvious to me that I could not improve on it. For this reason, I'm sharing the tale here as Henry Wiltse originally wrote it down.

"Turkey Story: First One Stolen"
By Henry Wiltse

This slight deviation from the conventional solemnity of history writing may seem frivolous, possibly digression, but it is neither. No, it is at the same time making a record of an actual occurrence in history, and keeping a promise. Using a phrase more familiar than elegant, this story is "all wool," but there is no yarn about it. In 1905 I met Mr. Weathers, an affable and sprightly man of eighty-one summers who had become interested in some history notes of mine, being published from day to day. On learning that I was the writer of them, he with the appearance of deep earnestness inquired: "Do you know who stole the first Turkey here in Chattanooga?" Being informed that I had not yet got around to that particular branch of the subject, and consequently did not know, he made avowal—"Well sir, I am the man."

Under the encouragement of several interrogatories and a cigar, he entered into details. He and a number of comrades had enlisted for service in the War with Mexico, and came down overland from Bradley County to join others and proceed by steamboat to New Orleans. The Bradley County boys were hungry upon arrival here, and stopped at a little eating house conducted by Mrs. Jenkins and her three daughters. While the fare was good enough, there was a dearth of fowls and their appetites made increasing demands for poultry. So obedient to such behest, Mr. Weathers and two others determined to go out foraging one night. Was this not a commitment to war; in truth a war measure of prime importance? To be sure.

They went, but neither saw nor conquered. Mr. Weathers, however, believed that he had discovered a fair prospect, good sign, as an Indian or native might have said. Excusing himself later he went out alone. Sure enough—he discovered a large, comely hen turkey in the very act of going to roost. Chattanooga turkeys had not yet been taught by experience, as they were later, the saving essentially of roosting high. The season did not seem to Mister Weathers fully ripe. The witching hour had not yet arrived. The psychological moment was in transit. Mister Weathers returned to the Jenkins home and informed his friends of his gallinaceous discovery. They held their first council of war. As one result they built a pine-knot fire. Soon Mister Weathers went back to see how the turkey was getting along. She was not getting along. No, she was right there and had apparently gone to sleep. Her awakening was a rude one. Mister Weathers grabbed her by her feet and grabbed her sans ceremony; grabbed her quite unsentimentally and unfeelingly, grabbed her without her knowledge or consent, and with utter disregard of turkey hen dignity as well as soldierly deportment, ran, made off, "broke" as he phrased it, but in point of fact, ran like a turkey, as also with a turkey.

The course of fowl theft did not run so smooth as Mister Weathers had anticipated. There was a disturbing element, an intervention, though not of the foreign brand. The owner of the fowl had discovered what was going on and in what direction. He called a halt, but Mister Weathers did not respond to the call. The owner had a gun and it was loaded. The owner fired at Mister Weathers, soldier though he was, and Mister Weathers ran all the harder. However he was not forming the habit. He did not carry the propensity with him to Mexico. As for the wound, he had about the same opinion of it that Mercutio expressed of his "'Tis not so deep as a well, nor so wide as a church door; but 'tis enough, 'twill serve." He felt that he could feel blood running from practically every pore of him, but it was not quite so desperate a case as that. He ran in every direction except the right one with the purpose of foiling his pursuer, and in this succeeded to a nicety. When he reached the house—worn, breathless, spent and dying, as he believed, a discovery awaited him. It was psychological and chemical, in strange combination. The blood that he had felt trickling down his person was a mixture of perspiration, perfervid imagination and uncontrolled fright. He had not been shot. The wound was in his mind's eye.

He ate none of the turkey. Indeed, according to his seemingly earnest statement he had never eaten any from that night in 1847 to the day in 1905 when we held our interview. His appetite for turkey went "glimmering with the dream of things that were" as he ran like a turkey with the turkey's claws in his hair and various parts of his flesh. He expected never to eat turkey again so long as life should persist. After his story had been concluded, Mister Weathers insisted with childlike simplicity and persistence that he should be given credit for having stolen the first turkey ever confiscated in Chattanooga. Who could deny so reasonable a request?

So here you have it—set down for posterity the story of a man and a misdeed and how the lesson learned through his crime served his later life well. What this all means to today's reader is very simple and apparent: don't try to steal a turkey in Chattanooga. The only time we eat turkey is at Thanksgiving now and none of us actually imagine a live turkey when Thanksgiving dinner comes to mind—times have changed, of course—but the underlying lesson carries well into our modern times. All I feel compelled to add to the tale is a simple reminder: we would all do very well to honor the old adage that we should always learn from history and make ourselves a wiser people by honoring both the accomplishments and, perhaps even more importantly, the mistakes of those who came before us. Mr. Weathers committed a crime, and as a result, he lost his taste for turkey. He paid a dear price, yet he became a wiser man.

Old Mr. Weathers wanted his confession set down for the ages, and I, like Henry Wiltse, can see no reason to deny such a reasonable request.

BRONZE JOHN

It began with fevers and headaches. Some complained of nausea and said they felt dizzy—when they stood up, they vomited. Sometimes these symptoms passed after a few days. For most people, they didn't. They became worse.

Small children had seizures. People bled from their noses and mouths. Their lower stomachs swelled, and they couldn't relieve themselves. They were in pain. Their fevers rose higher, and they became confused. Nobody knew what was wrong. Their heartbeats grew slow. Women bled from between their legs and began vomiting black blood. Their bodies stank, and their skin turned yellow. The fevers rose even higher, and their heads were on fire. People came in and out of comas and moaned in bloody, soiled sheets. It wasn't until they started dying that a Louisiana doctor finally made a diagnosis: they all had yellow fever.

Yellow fever—or Bronze John, as people called the disease—came on a boat from Cuba that landed in New Orleans on May 23, 1878. Three months later, the people of New Orleans were in a panic and began fleeing north.

The fever followed them. It traveled by boat up the Mississippi River to Memphis. When confirmed cases were reported in Memphis, the locals fled by the thousands. As many as fifteen thousand terrified refugees headed east toward Nashville. But word of their deadly affliction had preceded their arrival, and Nashville told them to stay out. Fleeing refugees would not enter their city, they said. Nashville would not harbor them, and those attempting to enter the city would suffer severe consequences.

One early morning, Thomas Carlile, Chattanooga's mayor in 1878, brought his town leaders together and told them that something must be done. Chattanooga's generous spirit and strong vitality demanded action, he said, and human decency would not allow his city to stand idle while such suffering ravaged Chattanooga's southern neighbors. The time for action had come.

That very day, Mayor Carlile sent a handful of healthy young boys out to old Market Street. These boys hollered on the corners and handed out fliers to passing citizens. A meeting was to be held that night for the purpose of instituting relief measures for Memphis, New Orleans and other cities that had been struck by Bronze John. The message on the fliers read:

NOTICE!

In view of the suffering prevalent among our countrymen in New Orleans, Vicksburg, Memphis and elsewhere from the ravages of Yellow Fever, it behooves those whom a merciful Providence has preserved in health and comfort to lend a helping hand to their suffering brethren.

Chattanooga, noted for its energy and public spirit in its home interests, should not be slow in taking action. The city leaders call on their fellow citizens, one and all, to meet at

James Hall

Monday, Aug. 19, 1878, at 8 o'clock, to take steps to assist in sending aid to the sufferers from the fever. Come out! Our brethren need our help.

The foregoing call was hastily prepared late this morning. A full attendance is earnestly desired.
Chattanooga, Aug. 19, 1878.

Another flier, describing the situation more graphically, was handed out to Chattanooga citizens three weeks later:

The terrible suffering of our brethren at Vicksburg, Memphis and elsewhere, is only too well known. Strong men, tender women, helpless children, alike fall victims. Sick ones die sometimes unattended, and bodies at time lay unburied for days. All over the country the charitable are sending relief, but there is yet much to be done, and terrible suffering may be expected for long and weary weeks, until the frost comes, and we whose homes have been spared should not be slack in giving.

Learning that cities such as Nashville had refused to harbor the wandering sick, Mayor Carlile declared Chattanooga a haven for the stricken and afraid.

His city's doors were open, he declared, and the newspapers invited all who sought refuge.

The climate here was much too mild for an outbreak of yellow fever, the Chattanooga newspapers declared. We were protected by our unique climate and our surrounding mountains, it was said. Our altitude is much too high. The Chattanooga landscape was believed to be an impenetrable protection against the deadly disease. The newspaper advertised "Simmons Liver Regulator," "Seabury's Sulfur Candles" and the "Iron and Alum Mass," all of which were said to further bolster Chattanooga's immunity to the disease. Most importantly, the daily paper boasted, was that Chattanooga had been blessed by God, and because of this and in no small part our peculiarly healthy climate, we had nothing to fear. Messages were quickly sent out to Chattanooga's sick and ravaged neighbors, saying, "Come one, come all!" Take refuge and find safety with us!

The desperate refugees wasted no time in accepting Chattanooga's gracious offer. Almost five hundred arrived from Memphis in a matter of days. They were given room and board, were fed and were congratulated on having made it to the safe haven of Chattanooga. Mayor Carlile saw no reason to have his city doctors examine these incoming refugees or keep them separate from the healthy locals. The city's high altitude and healthful climate would not allow the virus to thrive, he was once again assured, and Chattanooga citizens were safe from any threat of Bronze John. Instead, Mayor Carlile insisted that Chattanooga concentrate on raising money for the cities in the Mississippi valley and offering helping hands to the poor refugees who were arriving daily. Mrs. Carlile, the mayor's wife, took to the city streets herself to ask for money, hoping to set an example for Chattanooga's everyday citizens. She went from merchant to merchant and from person to person on the city streets. Mrs. Carlile even went bravely into the bars and saloons down along the riverbank and found charity even among the derelicts and drunkards. The mayor's wife was widely praised for her selfless works, and the newspapers proudly told her tale. Chattanooga was a beacon of "Hope, Health and Charity," they said, and because of so many acts such as those of Mrs. Carlile, divine providence would continue to uphold and strengthen this light on the hill.

But just a few days after the first refugees arrived, in a house on the corner of Eighth and Cherry Streets, a woman died. She was a Jewish woman who had fled Memphis. Bronze John had crawled into her before she arrived in Chattanooga, and the city's healthful climate had been unable to sustain her. Her body was hastily buried and her clothing and belongings burned.

Disturbed murmurs went through the city, but Mayor Carlile immediately sent out word that yellow fever would never become an epidemic in

Chattanooga. The city's climate would not allow it, the newspapers said. Those who were now sick and beginning to die were already infected with the virus when they arrived, the public was told. These cases were isolated and were not a threat to the well-being and health of Chattanooga. Preachers and priests agreed—a preacher named Bachman stood on McCallie Avenue every morning to reassure and comfort the citizens of the city. He began each morning by reading aloud the Ninety-first Psalm—"Surely He shall deliver thee from the noisome pestilence"—and spent the rest of the day reminding everyone that they should not fret or despair. Despite the Jewish woman's death, God and the cool mountain air were on our side, and with such allies, Chattanooga was safe from all harm.

Dr. R.N. Barr, a former Union army surgeon who had treated yellow fever before, said that all these people were fools. Bronze John was here, he said, and he was loudly persistent that quick action should be taken to protect the citizens of Chattanooga from the deadly virus. The sulfur candles and "liver regulators" were ridiculous, he said. Death was on its way, and the providence that was being so loudly and highly spoken of would soon turn to a curse the likes of which the city had never seen. But Dr. Barr was laughed at, called a rabble-rouser and a fool by the city doctors and harshly admonished by city authorities. This Dr. Barr called them all fools again and immediately left town.

A refugee camp was established in the city. Little refugee children and their families were given homes there. Local citizens paid hospitable visits to the camp and welcomed the sick families to town. A young Chattanooga boy named Cory lived nearby. He often went to the refugee camp to play with the newly arrived children. It was okay, everyone smiled and said. All our little children are safe. But after playing with the other children, little Cory became sick, and in a matter of days, the little boy was dead.

But "the air in the night is too cool here to allow the fever to spread," it was said once again. The *Chattanooga Daily Times* ran an editorial insisting that citizens stay calm and to not "fret yourselves into a fever. Above all, don't rush about creating alarm among the weak and timid. Let us assure all that everything is being done that science, experience and prudence dictate to assure the health of the city, which is remarkably good; better than it has been at this time for many years. Excepting a few cases of the fever, there is absolutely no sickness. Shall our people run from a figment of imagination?"

Disregarding the reassurance offered by the newspaper editorial, a small number of families followed Dr. Barr out of town anyway. They packed a few quick things, boarded their homes shut and made their way north. Most stayed home, though, and were thankful that they lived in a place as safe as Chattanooga. They believed what the newspaper said, and they trusted their mayor, local doctors and city leaders. The men in the saloons drank and laughed. Children played in the streets, and their mothers cooked and went about their daily chores. The fathers worried a little but continued to work, and Mayor Carlile rested in his mansion, smoked cigars and played billiards.

Then a local black man died. Then another. The refugees in the camp began dying one after the other, and another little boy died. This poor little boy's mother also died after trying to nurse her child back to health. A healthy, thirty-five-year-old white bricklayer died. The skin of these dead was yellow, and their mouths were bloody. Their deaths were sickening, and the bodies stank. Others began feeling sick all around town, and Chattanooga panicked.

It was here.

People immediately began fleeing the city in droves. Their pathetic attempts to escape Bronze John resulted in chaos. Every boat and train leaving the town was full of frightened families seeking refuge anywhere they could find it. Horses and mules were saddled for those who could not afford passage on the water or the rails, and in a matter of days, the population of Chattanooga was reduced by 90 percent.

Bronze John crawled through what was left of the town, and death became everything it touched. Yellow fever was an indiscriminate sickness and struck man, woman and child, regardless of race, creed or social worth. The death caused by yellow fever was normally prolonged and agonizing. This was not always the case, however; some who caught the disease died within hours. The *Daily Times* later told the story of a man named W.T. Monger who had gone from being in good health to yellow and dead over the course of a day:

> *Mr. Monger was standing on the corner of Eighth and Market Streets when he was met by a man named Charles George.*
>
> *"Charley, I've got it," said Mr. Monger. After a look at him, Mr. George concluded that this was true, and advised the sick man to go at once to his home near the corner of Eighth Street and Georgia Avenue.*
>
> *"No," said the infected Mr. Monger, "I am going to die on my feet."*

Mr. George eventually succeeded in persuading Mr. Monger to go home and accompanied him to his front gate. From there, Charles George hurried across town in search of a doctor. He found one without much delay. The two started in haste for Mr. Monger's home but again found him at the corner of Eighth and Market Streets, near where Mr. George had first seen the sick man. Mr. Monger was now violently crazy and determined to walk until the end—to die on his feet. Mr. George followed and watched the madman stagger through the city for over an hour before he fell dead and yellow on the side of the street.

Deaths such as that of W.T. Monger were occurring all over the city. Mayor Carlile decided that he could not allow the dead to fill Chattanooga's streets this way. He set up quarantine areas and ordered those who were sick to stay within those confines. Those who became sick were ordered into these "pest houses," as they were called. If they were in their homes and refused to go, they would be forcibly removed. The welcome song Chattanooga had sung quickly changed, and new messages were sent to refugees seeking harbor within Chattanooga's healthful climate:

NOTICE!
A SEVERE PENALTY FOR OFFENDERS AGAINST THE QUARANTINE ORDINANCE.

To Refugees From Infected Points, or Points Against Which Chattanooga Has Quarantined:

Chattanooga cannot, and will not, harbor you. Our health and security must be preserved, and it is of the greatest importance to you not to start for this city, because you will in no case be admitted into the city limits. If by any chance you should get in, and your identity should become known, which will surely be the case, you will be arrested and detained for fifteen days in a Yellow Fever quarantine station and suffer the severest penalty of the city ordinances. And further, all parties in the city who may harbor such refugees will also be isolated and quarantined for ten days and fined. This rule is absolute, and will not be suspended on any account.

A relief committee was soon organized by Mayor Carlile to assist the sick and to help maintain order in the city. There was no fire department to speak of, as most of its members had fled. The police department was drastically reduced, and crime had become rampant. Violent crimes went unchecked—fighting and shootings occurred frequently and randomly. Looting and petty thievery seemed unstoppable. While neighbors and old friends were bleeding, suffering and dying of yellow fever and the charitable relief committee ran back and forth between the beds of the dying, looters stole from empty houses and storefronts were smashed.

Mayor Carlile decided that the theft and crime were intolerable and would be stopped, if hanging had to be brought in to stop it. Mr. "Eb" James was

Early image of Market Street, near where Mr. Monger died. *Library of Congress.*

The undertaker's building. *Library of Congress.*

given the job of acquiring lumber, nails and rope for the construction of a gallows. Mechanics and carpenters were found who were willing to do the job, and in a most conspicuous place in the heart of the city, the gallows arose.

The few policemen the city had left scoured the city for these looters and thieves. While they were doing so, a certain man preyed on their minds. This man was named Harry Savage. Harry had been wanted by the police for some time, but since the outbreak of yellow fever, there had been no time to spend trying to find him. Some assumed he had fled the city. Others, knowing Harry Savage as they did, simply could not imagine him running from so great an opportunity. The crime for which he was wanted was the deadly assault on a well-known businessman named J.W. Kelly. Harry Savage held Mr. Kelly at gunpoint and beat the man mercilessly. Harry was a professional gambler and gunman—a devilish outlaw, the newspapers said—and the lawlessness of the city in that time of misery and turmoil was the perfect working ground for such a lawless man. He was a desperado, everyone knew, and one who took pleasure in the misery he caused and the dangerous reputation he carried with him.

The more Harry crossed the minds of the city leaders and police, the more concerned they all became. They knew he was still in the city, and as usual, he was about some evil business. Some of the storefront smashing and the looting of the homes of the sick or dead were surely the work of Harry Savage. This man was thought to be so base, so self-centered and cowardly, that it was quite likely that he was the ringleader and mastermind behind all of the criminal havoc that was terrorizing the desperate town. The police set about trying to find him at once.

It didn't take them long. Harry was seen coming up and down the back staircase of a building in a prominent section of town. He came in and out of that city building often, always furtively and by way of a back staircase. He was up to no good, and the police finally had him. That police vengeance was set afire, and the instinct ran through the city-armed men like the mad instincts that run through a pack of wild dogs. The thought of how a man such as Harry Savage could use the misery and death of innocent others to such vile benefit turned their knuckles white, and madness and broken bones rang in their ears.

The police decided immediately that Harry Savage would be stopped. They were going to make an example of him. Those gallows would not have been raised in vain. The police set up surveillance on the building Harry was known to be hiding in and waited until they were sure he was there. Once they had him, the police stealthily climbed the building's back staircase and stormed inside.

The police found little children there—sick and dying yellow fevered little children. Little kids whose parents had either died from the fever themselves or had fled in cowardly terror and left their own children behind like infected clothes. The desperado Harry Savage had been going around the city and collecting these abandoned children. Harry carried each little child in his arms and up the back staircase of the building. He laid them on pillows and wrapped them in blankets in an abandoned room there. Harry had worked tirelessly and alone and was nursing these sick orphans as best as he could. Harry had been gathering food, water and whatever else he could find to ease the suffering of these sick orphaned babies. When the police saw what Harry Savage had been up to, they quietly left back down the back staircase up which they had just stormed up. Harry Savage was left by the police to continue his work until he contracted yellow fever himself. The desperado Harry Savage died in that abandoned upstairs room where he had carried those sick orphan babies.

It seemed that everyone was dying. As in the days of the black plague, young men pulled carts through the streets and shouted, "Bring out your dead! Bring out your dead!" The dead were dragged out in sheets or even by their dead arms and thrown onto the horse-drawn carts. They were pulled through Chattanooga's streets and out to the Citizens Cemetery, where holes were already waiting for them. At that old graveyard, they were unceremoniously thrown into mass graves and quickly covered with black dirt. When one hole was filled, yet another was dug, and the wooden carts continued on, the drivers again shouting through Chattanooga's streets, "Bring out your dead!"

The city was dying, and everyone who still believed in a gracious God was now praying for frost. It was thought that a solid frost would kill the fever…but when would it come?

A letter from those days, a sad letter signed by a man named W.I. Crandall and written to his long-grown siblings living in a northern state, tells a personal tale. It's a letter telling how an early Chattanooga businessman buried his poor mother, how he worried about the fate of his germ-sequestered daughters, how he watched when his beloved wife, Delia, was laid low by the disease and how he cried and howled for his wife as he himself lay sick with the fever:

My Dear Brother and Sister,

I propose now to give you a detailed account of the tragedy which has befallen us; and shall mail it when finished, for I am weak and easily tired. The Doctors disagreed for one month as to the nature of the disease which kept cropping out, after the deaths of four Memphis refugees in our city. None questioned what they died of, but many disputed the sickness which kept the public in a fever of excitement. We discussed the matter at home every day and whether to leave at once or wait until matters took more decisive shape was the problem we tried to solve. Mother had not been very well for a month—had refused doctors because she did not feel unwell enough for that, but Delia and I often talked it over. Still, Mother was regular in her daily affairs and kept a good appetite, so we did not interfere. But when we proposed leaving the

This page: The Citizens Cemetery today. *Author's collection.*

city on account of the threatening fever, she opposed it—did not believe in running away from disease—believed that the Lord would care and provide. Delia was somewhat of the same way of thinking. Our daughters were ready to go or stay as we decided. People here were frantic and were fleeing to the mountains and ridges and neighboring places as people would receive them.

Mother and Delia did not favor the way many had done—get a wagon; load it up and go until some place was found. They both preferred to remain where comfort and help could be had. But during those days of doubts and plans, two cases of fever broke out on opposite corners. I became desperate, and ordered each one to pack a trunk with clothing, for I was bound to get out—where I did not know.

It was September 24th. At 5 P.M. I took the train and went forty miles to Tunnel Hill, found a nice Manor house which I rented for one month or longer, also a cow, and on the 26th started back home, rejoicing in my heart of the splendid arrangements we had obtained. I planned to send them all to the Manor house on the noon freight, while I would get furniture and bedding ready and follow at 5 P.M. I jumped off the train and hurried to them, only to find Mother down with the Yellow Fever, and Delia acting as nurse all through the night. Can you imagine my feelings and the bitter thoughts of my heart! I found the girls had not been in Mother's room, but I could smell the fever in Delia's clothes.

You can scarcely believe it, but the terrors of Yellow Fever seem to crush out all love, duty and affection in the hearts of many persons. Parents have been known to desert their children, husbands their wives, and the natural home to be severed. It has happened in Chattanooga, it has occurred elsewhere—so certain is death to follow exposure. I was gratified to my very soul that when Mother was taken with the chill, she had a daughter who put her to bed and watched and soothed her through the night. It was death, but it was love and duty. In my own mind I felt we had chosen a line of duty which meant death to our household. I prayed for my family, my wife and children, and if death was to enter that my life might be the last so that I could minister to the loved ones around me.

Delia had been up all night and all day and supported Mother and by eight o'clock that night, was fairly broken down with fatigue and anxiety. I made her go to bed and I watched Mother through the night, giving medicines and keeping her covered up. So strong was the smell of the fever that I had often to get to the open air to keep down the nausea. Mother was old, and the fever upon her was rank and more offensive than upon younger persons, although bad enough in any case. In the morning Mother had a paralytic spasm. I called up Delia, fearing Mother's death was at hand. It proved otherwise, but it convinced us that all hope for Mother was gone. It was a slight spasm, but it killed all hope.

When the two Doctors called the morning of September 27th and heard my account of the night, they said she would linger possibly, but that the mark was set. Poor Mother, she knew us till the last, answered our questions, but when I asked her if she had any special messages to leave, she looked long and steadily at me, but never said a word or expressed a wish. Once on this day she smiled upon me, but said nothing.

Delia and I remained up the night. Mother had those awful spasms about once every four hours. Each one I feared would be the last, but she held strong. As she was liable to drop off at any moment I saw the undertaker in order to secure, if possible, a metallic case. So many were dying and mother was so tall I feared to delay. Had Mother not lingered twenty-four hours I should have failed, but he had some come by express and by speaking in time, I secured one.

Mother passed the night as well as could be expected. The 28th dawned clear and warm. This day Mother began to show the final struggles approaching. The drooping chin, the languid eye, lack of recognition, the feeble moans, all told the dissolution approaching, and at eight P.M., after seventy-four hours from taking the chill she breathed out her life. It was a ghastly sight, especially under the gas light, never to be erased from my memory.

You may not know it but, but a dead Yellow Fever body in the house is a fearful danger. Decomposition begins before death and then advances rapidly. We obtained a black woman, a real Christian woman, to help us. Sulfur was kept burning in the room, the Undertaker and night wagon with two negroes arrived. I kept Delia from the room, but she stood by and directed the woman how to wind the body in blankets and sheets. This done the negroes put her in the case under my supervision and we carried her out the front window. We cemented the case carefully, and then with a lantern, alone at midnight, I went to the cemetery, and saw her safely laid away in a good part of the ground. It was a solemn and lonely trip to that burial spot. I could not stop to think, or weep, on account of the dark future.

In the morning, September 29th, Delia and I were alone. I noticed that Delia ate no breakfast. She was tired and worn out and felt uneasy about herself. Oh, you cannot imagine the anxiety of my heart as I watched her movements then. During the day I had been repeatedly all over the city for help, nurses, and doing the errands for a sick house; but when I realized that Delia was coming down, it was only by monstrous efforts that I could control myself. I persuaded her to take a warm bath, with alcohol and water, undress and have a good sleep. She consented, and I fixed her in bed, and prayed to God to give her a quiet sleep of restoration.

With the help of our Pastor I succeeded that day in securing two excellent nurses, one for night and one for day. One Mrs. Gledhill had had the fever about a month before. The other nurse was Miss Hattie Ackerman, a school teacher, a noble lady at heart, about thirty-five years of age to forty years of age. At the outset of the Yellow Fever epidemic she volunteered to be a nurse.

On September 29th at noon Delia awoke. Just then a Doctor came in. Delia sat up in bed and said, "Doctor, you have another patient." She spoke pleasantly, but to me it was agony. She had slept so sweetly and so long that

I had hopes that she would be spared. My prayer to be the last to die had been answered so far. I was still there to administer to my Darling. I took full charge of Delia with the advice of the nurse to aid me in doubts.

Delia's case was pronounced "light and favorable." She was brave, bound to get well—was cheerful. I gave her milk beef tea. For two days and nights I watched over her, feeling that although fleshy, her prospects were good.

About four A.M. October 1ˢᵗ, Delia went to sleep. Having been up four nights and days with only three hours sleep, I dozed off in the rocker beside her bed and did not wake until six A.M. Delia was awake and a Doctor had come in. He was pleased with Delia's condition. It was her fourth day. After the Doctor left I began to feel uneasy about myself and checked my pulse and lo it was thumping away about 110 a minute. I knew at once what it meant and came in and told Delia my turn had finally come. She was doing so well that we both thought we should go through. I immediately got a small box and gathered all our jewelry, watches, purses and small valuables together, disinfected each and putting a new ten dollar bill, four silver dollars and a half into my pocket book, gave it to Delia who put it under her pillow. I thought she was getting on so well that she would be up first and might need money.

I got another mattress into the parlor myself, hunted up my bedclothes, had a fire made, and then went into Delia and told her about my visit with the girls. I told her I was going to race with her to see which of us would get better first, and I kissed her goodbye. I never saw her more. Had I suspected this I would have lingered longer by her bedside, but she was doing so well—was still so brave.

I then made up my bed, and undressing, tried to sleep. This was noon October 1ˢᵗ. I prayed to God to spare my life for the sake of Delia.

The Doctor assigned Miss Ackerman to Delia and Mrs. Gledhill to me. Delia went through the night well. I was kept in perspiration with half hour naps, taking hot teas and medicines every half hour. I was so worn out that at first sleep was easy.

When I was fairly awake in the morning, they told me Delia was all right and getting on well. So I felt encouraged, but after a while I began to think it was not so, for my nurse was away a good deal, and I conceived many horrors, and finally I sent for Miss Ackerman and begged her to tell me about Delia. Then I learned how that strange feeling had run through her back and she began to doubt her chances to get well. I was then very sick, but not so that I was alive to her wants. I sent my love to her, told her not to despair, that I was doing well, and to pray for hope and strength. It cheered her up through and through the day until about four P.M. she was supposed to be doing well. About 6 P.M. the Doctor came and for two hours he and the nurses had a serious time with her. I made Miss Ackerman promise to keep me closely posted as to her condition. She told me that Delia felt sure that she could not get well—the suffocating feeling about her heart admonished her, that unless something could be done to relieve that, her hours were numbered.

How can I relate what my thoughts were? Soon it all flashed upon me—Delia's splendid constitution, resolution and habits were to be of no avail. Paralysis of the heart from the coatings of fat with a deadly fever at work was imminent and liable to prove suddenly fatal at any moment. I saw it all too vividly and I began to grow restless. I pictured her dead and began to lose control of my mind. My fever increased and I went crazy. I began to rave they said, and to struggle. They sent to the Nurse's home for help. A man nurse was sent and through that horrible night I fought the nurse and the two men who tried to quiet me. During all that fearful night Miss Ackerman was watching Delia, bathing her in whiskey and warm water and trying to relieve her breathing.

I know not in what condition I was, but I think I was in delirium when at four A.M. October 3rd my Darling turned upon her side and died.

At seven A.M. I had become rational and found strange faces about me, giving me a foot bath. The Doctor came and said my case was hopeless—past all relief. I knew nothing about it—cared less. I asked for my wife. Miss Ackerman had come in. she said my wife was dead—gone home to glory. I asked if she was buried. She said they had prepared her nicely and that a suitable coffin had been found and all was ready. Life was nothing to me. I wanted to die. They said I was a sorrowful sight. All I knew was that about ten or eleven o'clock I revived again and they told me Delia was buried—her body was taken by hearse to the cemetery and she was laid beside Mother.

In a dreamy way the Heavenly Vision, and the yearning plea of those remaining filled my soul and with all the power I could command I prayed to My Father to hear me, even then hovering on the edge of life and death, and spare me for my children's sake, and stay the "pestilence that walketh in darkness" which had smote us so heavily, and to restrain the remainder of the wrath. I was so weak that the only way I could remind myself of the situation was to call my left hand my children and my right hand myself and by moving my fingers I was reminded of the work before me.

I told my nurse I was bound to conquer and she must help, and she felt encouraged. I became quiet and studied myself. I made the Doctor tell me my temperature and my pulse (he called regularly three and four times a day). I asked the Doctor if bathing me every half hour through the night was not best to get the fever down. He agreed, and so that night (two days had gone since Delia died) I was rubbed with hot water and soda, and each time I slept about an half hour and we kept it up all night and on the morning of October 7th my temperature was lowered two degrees.

The Doctor came and was astonished at the result. This was the turning point for me.

Miss Ackerman attended Delia after I was taken ill. Delia took the fever September 29th 9 A.M. and died October 3rd 4 A.M. She was sick about 91 hours. I was with her 48 hours—Miss Ackerman the balance. Before coming here she had nursed a mother, child and someone else. She rested one night after leaving us, then nursed a Mrs. Bell Gledhill, a strong Irish woman who caught the fever of her neighbors whom she was helping and whom the Doctors said had no Yellow Fever. They did, though, for five of the family of seven died.

When Delia died the effects of the room and the drawers were locked up. My pocketbook was found by Mrs. Gledhill and the Doctor, in the presence of all three, ordered the pocketbook to be given to Miss Ackerman and locked up in one of the drawers. When I was able to get about the house I found the keys and my pocket book minus thirteen dollars. Miss Ackerman would never have taken it—nor do I think Mrs. Gledhill, but I think her husband did. He is now dead and the amount is small, so I concluded to say nothing. Other things are missed. Several families have been robbed, who having died, left premises thus exposed. Last night two men tried to enter Mr. Austin's house, supposing it unoccupied like most of the houses in town, but he was too much for them.

Tonight promises to be cold (the 17th). The Telegraph reports a cold snap at St. Louis and Storm. Today it has rained hard and cleared off the cold. I shall set up late and if there indicates frost I shall spread some bedding out. I have been fumigating the house and had a woman washing for three days, who also comes tomorrow. Our house was all pulled over, three nice mattresses, pillows, bolsters, sheets and blankets for three beds have all been burned. Thus you see how it goes.

October 18th. No frost last night—Thermometer 43 degrees. The girls well. Professor Underwood, Principal in the City High School, for whom Miss Ackerman was assistant, died last night of Yellow Fever.

This is a long letter, but I presume it will explain to you the state of matters and may be of interest. When I am able to look into business and get affairs straightened up, and strength, I will take up Mother's matters. I shall fumigate those sheets.

Yours Truly,
W.I. Crandall

Stories such at this man's occurred in every home that had not been abandoned, behind every door. The newspaper had long since stopped telling everyone to get over their fears and worries and began printing prayers to

God for cold weather to come. One newspaperman published this invocation to Jack Frost, the only entity believed to have the power to stop Bronze John's deadly curse:

> *While cities wail his deadly stroke;*
> *Trade bends beneath his rod,*
> *Praised our every interest lies;*
>> *Tears, bitter tears, suffuse our eyes,*
>> *Our bosoms burst with groans and sighs.*
> *Come, then, thou angel of the skies,*
>> *Thou messenger of God.*

When God didn't send Jack Frost as soon as was hoped, the *Chattanooga Daily Times* said it was because he worked in mysterious ways. All through the summer and through the first months of autumn, Chattanooga groaned, wept and wailed—more and more died each day—and it seemed that the God everyone prayed to was not listening to their prayers.

But at long last, on the night of November 4, 1878, a heavy frost blanketed Chattanooga. The city rejoiced—never before had a people been so overjoyed by a cold frosted morning. It was not the Second Coming, but it did seem miraculous when Bronze John was sent crawling back to the warmer southern climes from which it had come. The city authorities sent out word to those who had fled that the scourge had been lifted and that it was now safe to return. They were wary at first, but eventually they came home. A few cases lingered, and a few more people died, but by Christmas, the people of Chattanooga sat around fires in fireplaces and thanked God for the return of their health, their families and their homes.

Many years later, science and reason discovered that yellow fever was not a pestilence sent by the devil or a curse sent down from God. It was not a weightless germ blown along by the wind. It was a disease carried by a creature known as *Stegomya fasciata*—a mosquito. The old newspapers and city leaders had proclaimed Chattanooga to be a refuge from the disease because of its high altitude, but as a reporter recalled those days in a 1978 issue of the *Chattanooga Times*, it was pointed out that

> *the city, in fact, was probably an ideal breeding ground for the carrier mosquito. Unsanitary sewer conditions existed; unpaved streets were pocked with large, water-filled holes near which local pranksters placed signs such as "Good*

*Fishing Here"; and a frequently flooding river created swampy conditions.
People from other cities sneeringly circulated this ditty:*

Nashville is a fine old place;
Knoxville is a beauty.
But if you want to see a mudhole,
Just go to Chattanoo-gee.

After determining its source, science was able to rid the world of the terrible scourge of Bronze John. But the discoveries of science came too late for those who called Chattanooga home in the summer of 1878. Many of them had long since been buried in the mass graves in the Citizens Cemetery, their clothing burned and nearly everything they'd ever touched destroyed or bleached. The only thing left of those dead is a list of faceless names in a gray filing cabinet on the third floor of Chattanooga's downtown library. To read through the names of those unknown men, women and children is to hear the dreadful call of the horse-driven cart rattle once more through Chattanooga's muddy streets and to hear its tired driver again shouting, "Bring out your dead."

In one of those files, there is another letter. It is as sad as the letter left by W.I. Crandall, but it adds something to the tale. It was written by the same young Chattanooga schoolteacher who had nursed Mr. Crandall and had soothed his wife in her last dying moments: Miss Hattie Ackerman. Hattie was a selfless and humble woman who, as soon as the deadly scourge began, insisted on becoming a yellow fever nurse. Some said that she was the first to volunteer. Her friends begged her not to put herself at such risk. They pleaded with her to leave the city and return once the deadly threat was over, but Hattie refused. It was her duty, she said, and in her prayers, God insisted that she stay and help care for the sick.

This she did, and she was "run ragged" in her work. She denied herself every comfort and spent all her waking hours at the bedsides of her dying neighbors. Hattie watched death grow all around her, and there came a point when she knew that she, too, had been touched by Bronze John. She caught it while cooling fevers and changing the wet sheets of dying strangers. When she felt Bronze John crawling through her own body, she resigned herself to the sickening death against which she had fought so hard. During one of her final nights alive, the young schoolteacher sat down at a desk and wrote this last letter to one of her close friends. Despite the dumb absurdity and meanness that is always present when a people are looked at as a society, Hattie Ackerman's last letter reminds us that people and societies are made up of solitary persons, and because of some of these solitary individuals, goodness always prevails. It was not Mayor Carlile's threat of the gallows, the swarming diligence of the city police or the old doctors that sustained Chattanooga during the time of yellow fever. It was individuals such as the desperado Harry Savage and the schoolteacher Miss Hattie Ackerman:

My Dear Friend:

When you open this I shall be safe from all care, or sorrow or danger. I want to ask a favor of you to whom I owe so much. You cannot think how much I have appreciated your kind care for me, and what a haven of rest your home has been. God will bless you for it all.

Please give my clothes that are not destroyed to the poor, also my school books. If I leave any clothes that are not suitable for the poor, let them be sold for the benefit of the Orphan's Home.

I would like my watch and chain sent to my niece Hattie Lount, at Prescott, Arizona. To my niece Miss Emma Landon, send my cuff buttons and pin. I want her to have the sugar bowl and ice cream pitcher my mother went to keeping house with, also my grandmother's sugar bowl. They are with my sister. Give my writing desk and large Bible to May Wilder.

I have a note or acknowledgement for $75 in the Discount and Deposit Bank with two vouchers for $50 each. The balance of that and the unpaid salary for this month will bury me; or if the city I have served chooses to bury me, give that money to the Women's Christian Association, together with my sewing machine.

Ask Mr. Loomis to accept my hammock. It is at Mr. Tyler's. Somewhere in my trunk or boxes is a small gold pencil with a garnet in the end. Give it to your little daughter Jessie. Divide my ferns and mosses between Mr. A. Burns and Mr. T. Richmond. I promised them some, from Roan Mountain.

There is a log cabin built at Mr. Campbell's, into which I sewed some happy thoughts and bright hopes of a home of my own someday, years and years ago. Please keep it and all the odds and ends I have accumulated.

Please write my father for me and tell him of my fate. His address is B.P. Ackerman, Oxford, Michigan. Tell him I died doing my duty, and that I would rather my body should lie in Chattanooga, the home of my choice.

Yours lovingly,
HATTIE ACKERMAN

Friday, Sept. 27, 1878.

THE GREAT FLOOD

Water pourin' into Vicksburg, don't know what I'm gonna do
"Don't reach out for me," she said,
"Can't you see I'm drownin' too?"
It's rough out there,
High water everywhere.

—*Bob Dylan*

Early in the first week of March 1867, rains came and did not stop for four days. People looked out their windows and watched as Chattanooga's streets turned to mud and outlying crops were destroyed. The small streams and rivulets that ran off the sides of the mountains turned to raging rivers, and most troubling, the river was rising—sometimes at the terrifying rate of one foot per hour. Those who had the means made for higher ground, and those who did not held on.

The Military Bridge, then the city's only bridge across the river, became a gathering place for curious spectators watching the wild river rage. A large crowd became attracted to the devastation being rent upon the city. This crowd gathered on the Military Bridge to watch what the swollen river was washing out. They covered their heads, pointed at the water and talked excitedly about the terror falling from the sky. But soon, weakened by the force of the uncontrolled river, the wooden bridge began to creak and sway. The people in the crowd looked at one another and the wooden planks beneath their feet. When a loud *snap* was heard, they broke into a panic. They ran back to the riverbank and then turned to watch the great old Military Bridge on which they had just stood crumble into the raging river below. The city was now disconnected from the north shore of the river, and those curious watchers all ran back home. Things had become serious.

A telegraph from Knoxville came through to Chattanooga's telegraph station, asking if floodwaters had entered their city buildings yet. They had not. Knoxville said that they would by morning. Soon thereafter, all the telegraph wires were washed down, and communication to and from the city was cut off. Chattanooga was slammed by a river that had risen fifty-seven feet.

Homes and cabins floated down the widened river, and helpless, dying cries were heard from inside them as they passed. Once operable flour mills and corn mills floated down the river, as did water wheels, homes and livestock. The rail yard was

Episcopal church near the site where a boat capsized during the flood. *Author's collection.*

completely submerged. Maclellan Island was lost below the bridge like it was never there. A man farming on the island barely escaped. He made dry ground by jumping in the river and holding on to the horns of a swimming cow.

Boats paddled up and down Market, Broad and Chestnut Streets and on all the intervening streets as far south as what is now Martin Luther King Boulevard. One of these boats was seen capsizing between the Episcopal and Presbyterian Churches near Seventh Street, killing the three men who were on board.

Between nine and ten o'clock on Saturday night, splashes and cries were heard from two men in the water on Broad Street, just outside the Read House. Hotel guests heard them from the windows. The splashes and desperate screams for help from the two men stopped after a few minutes, and only the whispered sound of the water was heard. The Read House guests looked at one another in silence. They had learned what death sounds like.

Another house floated through the city near where Sutlertown once stood with two other men hanging on to its roof. The men slipped off. When they tried to climb back onto the roof, the house turned over, dragging the men to their deaths beneath it.

The bodies of countless other men, women and children all floated through the city—one man claimed to have been inside his house on the old Lookout Mountain road and watched as many as fifteen bodies pass before him one day.

During the night came the fiends. Windows were smashed and businesses were looted, their goods paddled silently away down the city streets. Homes were robbed, and an angry group of business owners, about one hundred of them, banded together and made their way to the commander of a military post then in Chattanooga, demanding that martial law be declared to stop the looting.

One afternoon, despite the dangers, an unknown but enterprising man rowed a barge from the river up Broad Street and into the Read House. This man paddled right through its front doors and welcomed aboard a band of fine ladies stranded at the hotel. This forgotten man toured the women through and around Chattanooga's Venice-like streets and showed them the devastation in progress. The visiting women were said to have very much enjoyed the ride, and this led to a new pastime for the next few days. Boats were constantly rowing through the doors and into the front room of the Read House and other city buildings, ferrying visitors about the crumbling town. Soon the city mayor put a stop to the spectacle, hoping to preserve the dignity of the dead and helpless.

In the very midst of all this terror and foolishness, even while the water was still rising, an anonymous reporter wrote the following to the desperate, flooded citizens of Chattanooga on March 9, 1867, in the *Daily American Union*, an old Chattanooga newspaper:

It seems, indeed, as though upon our fair land the curses of war, pestilence, and famine, were not sufficient, and now this additional calamity has befallen us. Still, one ought not to despair, nor to let their losses be an excuse for a folding of the hands and a cessation from labor.

This calamity should rather be an incentive to new efforts. So far as its being an injury to the future prosperity of the town is concerned, our citizens need feel no alarm. Under the direction of his Honor, Mayor Carr, our energetic and worthy Engineer, Col. Wm. B. Gaw, will, when this flood has reached its highest point, make a series of water marks, showing the height of this flood, and when the waters have subsided, and he establishes the grades of the streets in the city as he is authorized to do, the grade of every street in Chattanooga will be raised to a sufficient height above the level of this flood to preclude the possibility of any part of the city ever being again submerged. Chattanooga is a young and thriving city and, with all the chances in her favor, her people are not to be discouraged by anything. We are bound to make

this city the first city in the South, and by the help of God, who always aids
those who help themselves, we will do it.

Reading the accounts of the disaster today, one is struck by the absence of the sad stories. No writer spoke of angry tirades demanding the president come and part the waters. This was a different time. From the determined sound of those old newspaper stories, Chattanooga citizens of 1867 would have needed an even greater weather catastrophe before they cried out for help. Remember, the Civil War had just ended (in which Chattanooga had played a huge part), and Reconstruction was in its youth. For these drowning people to scream toward Washington, insisting that the federal government was responsible for their lives and livelihoods would have required a weather catastrophe along the lines of a cold day in Hell.

It was not until March 14 that the floodwaters began to subside, and the city was left covered in mud and debris and nearly destroyed. The *Daily American Union* told of the dangers being faced by downtown citizens and shopkeepers, of capsized boats leaning against storefronts, of a house washed up in the middle of Chestnut Street and of the wreckage of countless other structures strewn about the city. The newspaper also felt it important to offer this prudent warning to the unwary: "[H]oop skirts and unmentionable articles of women's apparel are seen hanging from drying lines in suspicious proximity to gentlemen's hats [and] coats." The *Daily American Union* left no stone unturned.

As the years passed, memories of the flood faded. The Tennessee River was dammed and brought under control. Eventually, the harrowing flood and the destruction of Chattanooga were forgotten.

More than a century later, archaeologist and University of Tennessee–Chattanooga professor Dr. Jeff Brown became fascinated by strange architectural features he was finding on some of Chattanooga's downtown buildings. Walking the city streets, he'd find the top of a window at sidewalk level here, a half-submerged doorway there. Asking around, he learned from some of the city's utility workers that there were tunnels beneath Chattanooga's streets, some of which ran all the way to the river while others led nowhere. There were stairways that led up to the sides of doorless walls. They told him about rooms beneath some of the older buildings that had been bolted and locked shut years ago, and no one could say what was on the other side.

Dr. Brown noticed that none of these tunnels or underground rooms was marked on any of the city's maps, and no one questioned seemed to know when they were created or why these mysterious tunnels and caverns existed. City workers told of digging outside downtown buildings and finding staircases that

A submerged doorway in a Chattanooga alley. *Author's collection.*

led into the sides of underground walls. Intrigued, Dr. Brown looked into these architectural oddities further, and what he eventually found was that the city of Chattanooga had been backfilled and lifted, from six feet at Ninth Street to more than twenty feet at the north end of downtown. Though forgotten, that anonymous reporter's exhortation in the March 9, 1867 edition of the *Daily American Union* had been carried out. The level of Chattanooga's streets had been silently raised, from the river all the way to Ninth Street, up to twenty feet at some points.

Strangely, the amazing feat was poorly documented. There were the newspaper reports and photographs of the flood, and then for nearly one hundred years, all was forgotten until Dr. Brown rediscovered, in a sense, the phenomenal task the citizens of Chattanooga had accomplished. While people were drowning and starving and the river still rising, they said they were going to pick the entire north end of the city up and raise it twenty feet—a nearly unimaginable task—but the proof of their determination and their accomplishment is found right under our feet.

The ruins are still there today. Under the streets and buildings on the north end of downtown, a person feeling ratty enough can pop down a manhole when no one's looking and see a side of Chattanooga that hasn't been seen in more than a century. Don't expect to find gold tombs, Dead Sea scrolls or Rosetta Stones there. There is wonder, though: staircases to nowhere, rusted metal lights hanging from rotten ceilings, doorways that lead to blackness, old signs painted and crumbling on walls that were once street level. These ruins are the dream homes of ghost stories, but the ghosts there are of a different

A submerged window that was once at ground level. *Author's collection.*

Alley steps leading to
a door beneath street
level. *Author's collection.*

A submerged doorway. *Author's collection.*

Tops of church windows that were once street level. *Author's collection.*

sort. You find under this city the ghosts of a time when men were determined to make it on their own and when self-reliance and pride determined a people's worth.

To today's citizens, the old 1867 mud puddle seems a thousand years away; to most it has been forgotten. But those old Chattanoogans who braved the Great Flood of 1867 lived through it and swore to restore the city that they were once proud of. Their city—the Dynamo of Dixie—was due a good bath, some of them laughed. They rolled up their pants legs, found their shovels and went to work. What if someone living today were to have passed by them then? Those early citizens would be standing in the middle of Market Street, knee-deep in mud and garbage, shovel in hand and sweating in the sticky air. They might pause for a moment if someone today were to pass by and ask them why the president didn't have the National Guard down there, or even why the president himself wasn't there to help clean up that pile on the north end of Broad Street. Those questions would most likely either draw a curse from the workers' lips or simply go unanswered. The questioner might have a handful of Chattanooga mud thrown at him.

Back in our world, the nightly news should remind us all that oil wells still explode, dams burst, economies bottom out, banks still don't give a damn about you and those bread lines are long. But twenty feet under the north end of Market Street, some mud-caked ghost might float up and remind a person of what citizenry once was and what self-reliance once meant.

It brings to mind a line from another song that Bob Dylan gave us. Those feeling so inclined can pinch their noses and tilt their heads back to achieve the right timbre and Dylan pitch, squint their eyes, point their fingers and in their proudest Chattanooga accent sing, "You get sugar for sugar and you get salt for salt and if you go down in the flood it's gonna be your fault."

HAYWOOD PATTERSON IS DEAD AND GONE

And when the evening mist clothes the riverside and the buildings lose themselves in the dim sky, and the warehouses are palaces in the night, and the whole city hangs in the heavens, and fairyland is before us—then the wayfarer hastens home; the working man and the cultured one, the wise man and the one of pleasure, cease to understand, as they have ceased to see…

—James Whistler

In 1931, the newspaper reported that Haywood Patterson was "one of the worst young Negroes in Chattanooga." The newspaper noted that Haywood and eight other black boys gang-raped two young white girls while riding a freight train out of Chattanooga. The paper added that Haywood was the ringleader and that he was an animal who wholly deserved the jailhouse execution that surely awaited him (he had not yet been to trial when the paper said this, thus the speculation).

Haywood was born in 1912. His father was a sharecropper on a farm in Georgia. That work was not much more than slavery, though, so when Haywood was still just a baby, his father moved the family to Chattanooga in the hopes of finding work in the city's steel mills. But the work wasn't there, and the family lived in squalor in what was not much more than a dog shack at the corner of what is now Main Street and Riverside Drive—the old black section of town that had always been near the river's edge until the threat of floods was taken away.

After moving to Chattanooga, Haywood said, life changed for him. On the farm in Elberton, all he knew was his younger brothers and sisters and all the small happiness that scampers around a farm. But in Chattanooga, he got to know city life, as much of it as there was in Chattanooga in the early

'20s. He made friends his own age from other segregated parts of the city. He visited Blue Goose Hollow and Tandry Flat. He walked over to the east side of Chattanooga to Bush Town, where black people with a little more money lived. He went swimming with his friends in the creeks around Alton Park.

His father eventually did find a job in a Chattanooga steel plant, the American Brakeshoe Company, and in 1924 and 1925, Haywood said that there was more money coming into his house than there ever was before. His father was earning forty dollars per week, and Chattanooga was being good to the Pattersons. Haywood got his first bicycle and rode it all around town.

But it didn't last. After 1929, his father's wage at the steel mill dropped to fifteen dollars per week, and the Patterson bellies started getting hungry. People were hungry all across the country then—the Great Depression had hit, and Chattanooga was not spared. Haywood tried not to eat at home so his sisters and younger brother would have more for themselves. He quit school and began making deliveries for a few local merchants to help bring money into the house. He rode from business to business up and down Market Street on his new bicycle, making deliveries and running errands for local merchants, but it wasn't enough. He was the oldest boy and felt responsible for his family—he wanted to help feed them. His youth and the hope that comes with being young drove him. "I wanted more," he said, "and faraway places were in my bones."

Haywood hopped his first train out of the Chattanooga rail yards when he was fourteen. As would any young boy, he reveled in the scary freedom that came with riding the tracks—not knowing where he was going and not knowing what he'd find. His was the American spirit chug-a-lugging through the dark and hot woods of the South, hoping that in the next town he would find what he was looking for. He rode those trains for years. He went as far south as Pensacola, Florida, as far west as Arkansas and north all the way to Ohio. "I could light a butt in the wind on top of a moving boxcar," he later boasted. "I had seen the main street of many a city, and always looked for a decent job. Always I had in mind the dream I would bring home some money for my parents, help them out."

Hoboing and hopping trains was simply what people in Haywood's predicament did in the days of the Great Depression. There were few cars and no public buses, and there was always the rumor of better work in the next city on. But by the time he was eighteen, Haywood still had not found any work. He always only found himself back in Chattanooga, empty-handed and hungry. But he refused to give up. On March 25, 1931, he and a few other like-minded boys hopped yet another freight train out of the Chattanooga rail yards, still hoping that something would come their way.

Years later, with the help of a newspaper reporter, Haywood wrote a book called *Scottsboro Boy*. In this book, he described what happened that day:

The freight train leaving out of Chattanooga went so slow anyone could get off and back on.

That gave the white boys [also riding the train] *the idea they could jump off the train and pick up rocks, carry them back on, and chunk them at us Negro boys.*

The trouble began when three or four white boys crossed over the oil tanker that four of us colored fellows from Chattanooga were in. One of the white boys, he stepped on my hand and liked to have knocked me off the train. I didn't say anything then, but the same guy, he brushed by me again and liked to have pushed me off the car. I caught hold of the side of the tanker to keep from falling off.

I made a complaint about it and the white boy talked back—mean, serious, white folks Southern talk.

That is how the Scottsboro case began... with a white foot on my black hand.

"The next time you want by," I said, "just tell me you want by and I let you by."

"Nigger, I don't ask you when I want by. What you doing on this train anyway?"

"Look, I just tell you the next time you want by you just tell me you want by and I let you by."

"Nigger bastard, this is a white man's train. You better get off. All you black bastards better get off!"

"You white sonsofbitches, we got as much right here as you!"

"Why, you goddam nigger, I think we better just put you off!"

Three or four white boys, they were facing us four black boys, and all cussing each other on both sides. But no fighting yet.

We had just come out of a tunnel underneath Lookout Mountain when the argument started. The train, it was going uphill now, slow. A couple of the white boys, they hopped off, picked up rocks, threw them at us. The stones landed around us and some hit us. Then the white fellows, they hopped back on the train. We were going toward Stevenson, Alabama, when the rocks came at us. We got very mad.

When the train stopped at Stevenson we got out of the car and walked along the tracks. We met up with some other young Negroes from another car. We told them what happened. They agreed to come in with us when the train started again.

Soon as the train started the four of us Chattanooga boys that was in the oil tanker got back in there—and the white boys started throwing more rocks.

The other colored guys, they came over the top of the train and met us four guys. We decided we would go and settle with these white boys. We went toward their car to fight it out.

I don't argue with people. I show them. And I started to show those white boys. The other colored guys, they pitched in on these rock throwers too. Pretty quick the white boys began to lose in the fist-fighting. Some of them jumped off and some we put off. A few wanted to put up a fight but they didn't have a chance. We had color anger on our side.

The white fellows got plenty sore at the whupping we gave them. They ran back to Stevenson to complain that they were jumped on and thrown off—and to have us pulled off the train.

The Stevenson depot man, he called up ahead to Paint Rock and told the folks in that little through-road place to turn out in a posse and snatch us off the train.

It was two or three o'clock in the afternoon, Wednesday, March 25, 1931, when we were taken off at Paint Rock...

Haywood didn't know there were two white girls dressed in men's overalls also riding the train. None of the boys did. These girls—Victoria Price and Ruby Bates—were cheap boxcar prostitutes and had been sleeping with other transients in the hobo jungle near the Chattanooga rail yard. When they, too, were pulled off the train, the girls said that Haywood and the eight other black boys had raped them. The boys raped them on a pile of rocks riding on a gondola car, the two girls said.

Haywood's mother found out about what happened to her son from the newspapers. The next time she saw Haywood, the southern courts had convicted him of raping those two girls and he was in a prison cell, waiting for his turn to die in the electric chair. He never found the work he was looking for and was never able to help his mama and daddy feed the family. And in those prisons, the hopeful young kid who had hopped a freight train looking for work one day was made into a prison-bred monster.

His hope and youth were beaten, kicked and starved out of him. Prison guards tied him up and whipped him like an animal. They held him down in a hole and beat him with fists and sticks and belts. When he spoke, they smacked him. They never let him see his mother again.

One prison guard paid two other inmates, friends of Haywood, fifty dollars to kill him. His friends beat him and stabbed him twenty times, puncturing one of his lungs and sending him to the brink. But Haywood wouldn't die.

On another night, the night Haywood was originally scheduled to die in the electric chair, he was forced to sit nearby as another inmate was fried in

The Lookout Mountain tunnel today. *Author's collection.*

the same electric chair in a nearby room. Haywood later described that night: "If I live to be a hundred I will never forget that day the juice was turned on in the death chamber. When they turned on the juice we could hear the z-z-z-z-z-z of the electric current outside in the death row. The buzz went several times. After the juice was squeezed into him a guard came out and gave us a report. 'Stokes died hard. They stuck a needle through his head to make sure.' I sweated my clothes wet."

Afterward, Haywood was made to carry out the dead man's body. "For a day or so I couldn't look into the Bible," Haywood went on. "But I held it so in my hands till from sweat the pages hung together."

As the years went by, death became an everyday part of Haywood's life. He gave up the Bible. The outside world slowly forgot about him. His innocence was lost, and his faith remained in only one thing. "I had faith in my knife," he said. "It had saved me many times."

Deprived of the company of women, he became sexually aggressive with other men, a "wolf" with his own "gal-boy," as the prisoners called them. A man in prison had to be one or the other, Haywood quickly learned, and he was bent on retaining his manhood. He beat a new, young prisoner into submission and made him his "kid." Later, he attacked another prisoner with a switchblade for trying to steal his young boy away. "He didn't try to take my gal-boy away from me after that," Haywood said. "Nobody did. And nobody tried to make a kid out of me no more. I had taken a gal-boy, whupped a wolf, and set myself up as a devil."

In 1933, after Haywood had been forgotten about and was fighting to stay alive in prison, a strange turn of events occurred in the outside world. One of the girls who claimed to have been raped on the train, Ruby Bates, had written a letter to her boyfriend. She gave the letter to a young man she knew and asked him to deliver it to her boyfriend. Her friend took the letter, but on the way he got into a fight with another young man and was arrested. Ruby's letter was found in the pocket of her friend by the police. A defense team that had been working for Haywood found out about it and demanded the letter be produced. The letter said:

Dearest Earl,

I want to make a statement too you Mary Sanders is a goddam lie about those Negroes jazzing me those policemen made me tell a lie that is my statement because I want to clear myself that is all too if you want to believe me OK. If not that is okay. You will be sorry some day if you had too stay in jail with eight Negroes you would tell a lie two those Negroes did not touch me or those white boys I hope you will believe me the law don't, I love you better than Mary does or anybody else in the world that is why I am telling you of this thing. I was drunk at the time and did not know what I was doing I know it was wrong too let those Negroes die on account of me I hope you will believe my statement because it is the gods truth I hope you will believe me I was jazzed but those white boys jazzed me I wish those Negroes are not burnt on account of me it is those white boys fault that is my statement, and that is all I know I hope you tell the law hope you will answer

After this letter was found, Ruby Bates confessed to everything. When they were found on the train, the girls made up a story about being raped by the black boys. "We'll go to jail if we don't say something," the older girl convinced the younger. The older girl was worried about being prosecuted under the Mann Act, which addressed taking minors across state lines for immoral purposes. When they were discovered on the train with Haywood that day, the girls told their fictional rape story to the Scottsboro police. But to the police and those old southern courts, none of this mattered. They didn't want to hear about the girl's confession, and Haywood remained in prison for the next fifteen years.

In the heat and drudgery of the days he spent working the prison cotton and cornfields, and in the dark and fitful nights he spent in his prison cell, Haywood slowly made up his mind to get out of prison. He adapted to the animal life of prison and became what he was forced to become, but that American sense of pride that sent him riding the rails hoboing in search of a better life for his mama, his underpaid daddy and his younger brothers and sisters, that determination, was now bent on the boy not dying at the hands of a prison guard or the electric chair. Society was never going to release him. So Haywood kept his head low, took the brutal beatings from the guards and waited for his chance to escape.

That chance came on July 17, 1948. He was taken with a gang of other inmates out to the summer cornfields of Kilby Prison. He waited until later in the afternoon, after even the guards had become tired from standing under that heavy southern sun. Haywood worked, but as he did, he slowly inched away from the guards and other inmates. He heard far-off train whistles blow. He was sweating, but he wasn't tending corn. That cornfield horizon was on his mind. Suddenly, an unexpected commotion stole the guards' attention, and Haywood's heart jumped. He made his break. He started running. He ran through the tall rows of unripe corn. He stumbled and fell and got back up and ran. He heard the prison guards hollering and his pounding breath coming out of his mouth. He listened for gunshots. He ran into the woods beyond the prison fields. The prison guards chased after him, firing those shotguns and calling for the dogs. He heard the other prisoners cheer him on, but this was not a feeding-time scrap. He was running for his life.

Haywood managed to avoid the guards and dogs that day and slept in the woods that night. Before sunrise, though, he heard the dogs on him again, and he started running. He had to elude the dogs for days. He backtracked toward the prison to throw them off his scent and tried walking through the middle of the prison farm's black, snake-infested creeks, but they stayed on him. He crawled out of the creek and ran toward a road that ran atop a small ridge on the outskirts of the prison grounds. He thought he'd take the chance of catching a ride on a passing truck but found the road lined with local police and prison guards, all of them cradling shotguns in their arms. There was nowhere else to run. If they found him, Haywood knew he would not be taken back to prison. They were waiting to kill him, and the dogs had him cornered.

He crept back to the black creek and waded out to a spot where the water was a little more than waist deep. He sunk down, holding only his head above the water, and waited for the dogs. He knew that he was no longer facing freedom or prison. It was life or death now.

The dogs' yelping got louder. He heard them coming. They found his scent, and by their cries he knew that they were close. He rose out of the water when the dogs jumped in after him. "When the first dog got to me I grabbed him, carried him under the water, and held him there till he stopped kicking," Haywood later said. "When I knew he was dead I turned him loose and he stayed under the water. I called after another. He swam after me. I carried him under the water. He was terrible. He was hard to die. He scuffled so he got his head up over the water." The third dog ran away.

But Haywood knew that the dog boys were close behind. He stayed low in the water and made his way farther down the creek, down to a bridge that was at the edge of the prison farm. He hid under that bridge, listening to the constant rumble of trucks and police cars searching for him on the road above his head.

He stayed under that bridge all day. Past the bridge was free people's land, and the next night, he began crawling toward that free land through the ditches alongside the road. He followed the road until he got to the railroad tracks that he still remembered well. He walked those tracks for miles, leaving them only to steal food from gardens along the way. He scurried down those railroad tracks like a scared 'possum. He only traveled when the sun was down, and he slept in the woods and underneath houses when it was bright outside.

When he felt like he was far enough away, Haywood hopped a train and hid in a toolbox just behind the engineer's compartment. He rode atop the jagged edges of the railroad tools from somewhere deep in Alabama all the way to Atlanta. In a rail yard there, he hopped another train and hid atop an open oil tanker for three hours. He felt a little bolder by then and let that free night wind blow over him. He watched the backwoods of the South pass by him in the night. When the train began to slow down, he recognized the river and hills around him. He climbed off the train and stepped off onto Market Street in downtown 1940s Chattanooga. He was home again. Haywood later said:

A Negro taxi was parked right there. I went up to the driver and I said, "Do you know Hal McCaffrey?" Hal was a relative of mine, a business man.

"I know Hal."

"I haven't got any money but if you take me to him he will pay. I haven't seen him in years and I have to see him."

"I'll take a chance. Get in."

I looked at Chattanooga late at night. The moon lighted things. The place looked strange to me, still familiar, but smaller, much smaller than when I left.

I was most nervous, noticing everything, not wanting anything to go wrong now.

The driver took me to Hal's café. It was in full bloom when I walked in. Many people there were having a good time and it seemed like everything went quiet when I came in. By me being so dirty-looking, my whiskers grown, they began laughing at me.

Market Street, circa
1940s. *Library of Congress.*

I walked up to my relative, a big-shot Negro in that town. He was behind the counter serving people. His wife was right there too, looking just as young as when I last saw her.

"Do you know me?" I asked Hal.

He didn't and I said, "Well, I'm going to try to make you know me. Did you ever know Claude Patterson and Jannie Patterson?

He knew them and when I said I was their son, he turned to his wife and said, "That's him."

"Just take it easy," I said, "and keep quiet. All I want you to do for me is to give me enough money to get to my sisters. About fifteen or twenty dollars."

He pulled out a roll, peeled off four fives, and gave them to me. Before I turned to go I said to his wife, Matie, "Don't say nothing."

"I won't say nothing."

I rushed out, paid the taxi man a dollar, and asked him to take me to a hotel, also to a place where I could get some drinks. I was in a bad state and needed something to steady my nerves.

He ran into a joint and got me drinks. Then he took me to a quiet place where I got some food. I looked pretty bad sitting there eating while the well-dressed people looked at me. The cabman waited outside for me. Then he took me to a hotel.

I paid him off and went inside to clean up. I didn't want a bad appearance to wreck things for me now.

I didn't stay long. I shaved, washed, drank a half pint of liquor, and came out of the hotel. Headed straight for the freight yards again.

I knew just what train to look for. Trains with numbers from 6300-6600 go to Kentucky and Ohio out of Chattanooga. It was the same as eighteen years before. I took train 6600 into Kentucky. Then jumped into Ohio, riding all that night, moving out of the South fast now.

I got off at Cincinnati. I beat it to a bus. A Negro minister was in there and I sat down by him. I told him who I was. He was glad and said he'd see me the rest of the way into Detroit.

A cab took me to 1973 Sherman Street, in Detroit, the home of my sister Mazell.

The day after I got there my sisters cooked a great home-coming meal. The first good family meal I had since I was a little boy. I tasted beer there for the first time. I was thirty-six years old when I had my first glass.

While in the city of Detroit, Haywood was involved in a barroom brawl that resulted in the death of another man. He was charged with murder this time, convicted of manslaughter and died in a Detroit prison on August 24, 1952, only three years after he'd tasted his first beer. That's who Haywood Patterson was. That's what became of that young boy's life.

I stumbled across Haywood Patterson's name while stomping through the woods around the bottom of Lookout Mountain. There is an old railroad tunnel there, near where the mountain meets the river. I walked a little ways into the tunnel and found old graffiti on its walls from the time the tunnel was being built, along with some old hobo tags from long ago. Fascinated, I looked further into the old tunnel's past. It was there that Haywood Patterson's name appeared. When I learned who he was, I was shocked and a bit embarrassed at myself for never knowing his story and his connection to Chattanooga before. I thought I'd let it all go, but something about the young boy, the tunnel and just the way Chattanooga can be sometimes haunted me for weeks. No one I spoke to knew who Haywood was. No one knew anything about the "Scottsboro Boys" or the fact that most of them were young Chattanooga boys hoboing for work when they found themselves in the old diabolical southern court system. Something seemed wrong—shameful, even.

One drizzly Monday morning, I walked through the streets downtown, determined to find someone who knew who Haywood Patterson was, or someone who would at least listen while I told his story. Incidentally, I was also working on a story about the homeless for a Chattanooga weekly paper at the time. So, to kill two birds with one stone, I walked out to the Chattanooga Community Kitchen, the place where the city's homeless go to eat. There were some papers I was to pick up at the front desk, and I thought that would be as good a place as any to look for someone who knew Haywood Patterson.

It was just after breakfast in the Kitchen, and the dayroom was crowded. All the chairs were full. A few old guys stood by the windows with bags of clothes at their feet, waiting for the wet rain to pass. A few others argued with a man in a monk's robe at the front desk about the distribution of cheap donated tents. I got my papers from the desk there and walked out into the dayroom.

In a back corner, a small crowd had gathered around two old black men playing checkers. The impromptu crowd huddled over the two men, clapping their hands, hooting and laughing like they were watching a chicken fight in some old backyard. I stepped close to one of the old men playing the checkers game and asked him if he'd ever heard of Haywood Patterson.

"Who?"

"Haywood Patterson."

"No, I ain't heard of him."

"He was one of the Scottsboro Boys…" Just then, the other player made a quick slick move, and the crowd around the two erupted in howls and laughter. The old man cursed his opponent, and I was shoved out of the way by the crowd of laughing men.

That was that, so I went back through the overcrowded dayroom to sit in a chair near the front door, waiting with the others for the rain to let up. Later that afternoon, I walked inside the Pickle Barrel, a pub down on Market Street. I ran into an old friend of mine there, a well-traveled girl who usually knows a lot more about these kinds of things than I do.

"You ever heard of Haywood Patterson?" I asked her.

"No. Was I supposed to?"

"Somebody's supposed to. He was one of the Scottsboro Boys."

"I've heard of them, but I can't remember who they were. There was a musical called the *Scottsboro Boys* on Broadway one time."

"Haywood Patterson was from Chattanooga. He grew up here in the '20s and '30s. He lived over near Riverside Drive down by the river. He was one of the Scottsboro Boys—the whole Scottsboro Boys thing started over a fight and argument in a railroad tunnel in the woods right over here by my house. In a tunnel I found right on the river side of Lookout Mountain. His story is terrible, but he was one tough…"

"Oh Lord. Here you go again." She pointed at me with her thumb and told the bartender, "He needs a beer." The bartender knew what to bring, and that was that, too.

A few more attempts to find someone in town who knew who Haywood Patterson was failed just as miserably. I hung around the pub until late afternoon. I talked about other things with my old friend for a few hours, but

Haywood Patterson stayed in the back of my mind. Why had Chattanooga forgotten him? Why had the city never once claimed him as one of its own?

I soon told my friend goodbye and walked over to the library. I spent the rest of the evening there, digging into Haywood Patterson's story. While there, I accidentally came across a letter he wrote from prison. He wrote it on October 20, 1937, to a young boy named Bobby while he was still in prison and waiting for his turn to die in the electric chair:

> *You Have two cute frogs and one is Expecting to Have babies. My How I would like to see those frogs. What sort of things is they? I am happy to Know that you all Have more kittens. And I can imagine How Beautiful they are, especially If they are very playful. Bobby dear, I Can Not Help but to love you awfully Because you seems Most Kind and considerate to the poor Helpless dogs and Kind to all things. you are Heavenly sweet to Have found a Home for the poor lost dog its good of you and I too Hope that the poor fellow will be nicely treated where ever he are. I feel very Sad for the poor Homeless dog. Honestly I do and am glad you all Had sympathy for Him and founded him a Home mighty nice of you. god will bless you for your Kindness to everything*

They soon called closing time at the library. I shut my notebooks and made my way outside. I sat on the steps in the dark outside the library, wondering if I was nothing more than some kind of ghoul dragging up the dead and buried for no other reason than my own curiosity. That letter to the young boy named Bobby was none of my business, and Haywood Patterson was dead and gone. His story was old. Nobody else seemed to give a damn anymore. Why should I?

The Pickle Barrel's lights were still on, and I could hear music and laughter spilling out of the bar. I still had friends there I could go see. I could have walked across the two streets and a parking lot that separated me from them and forgotten all the silliness I'd dug up.

But I couldn't help it. I felt haunted, like I had knocked on the door of a dead man and woken him. And since I had woken him, he was chasing me—pushing me deeper into his long-dead life. I walked down to the corner of Main Street and Riverside Drive where Haywood used to live. I needed to see the world from his perspective—to see what he had once saw with his young eyes. Although it has forgotten Haywood Patterson, Chattanooga hasn't changed all that much since he lived here. The mountain and river are still here. I wanted to see if I could find his old boyhood home. I wanted to see what Haywood saw when he was a child.

The small shack that he grew up in is not there anymore. Instead, there are brown brick housing projects on the corner of Main Street and Riverside. I stood on the corner there and looked up to my left. The rain had let up, though the clouds were still there, and lights from the big houses on Lookout Mountain shone against them. Old barges bellowed on the river, and fog was rolling up. A train whistle blew somewhere far off. Orange streetlights were smeared against the sky. I walked around the corner to where Haywood's house used to be and looked into the dark rows of the brown brick project buildings.

Chattanooga's Westside Projects on the site Haywood Patterson once called home. *Author's collection.*

I saw people watching me there. Some moved like shadows in the dark, and I couldn't see them. People stood under clotheslines that were in every backyard and said things I couldn't hear. In the shadows behind the streetlights, people moved. Everyone knew I was there. People I couldn't see knew I was there, and I was afraid. I was very afraid.

Freight train coming out of the Lookout Mountain tunnel. *Author's collection.*

I hurried back down the sidewalk, around the corner and out to the middle of Main Street. Once there, I ran. I ran down the middle of Main Street so people passing by in cars might see me. When I got closer to

Chattanooga's Westside Projects. *Author's collection.*

downtown, I ducked down alleys and behind bushes and dumpsters, taking every shortcut I knew to get back to where I belonged.

THE HOTEL PATTEN

Since its birth, Chattanooga has been known for the beauty of the scenery surrounding it. The river, the fog that rises off the water at night and the soft hills in the valleys have caused residents to swoon and brought visitors from many miles away. That soft blue-gray rise and then abrupt fall of Lookout Mountain into the river has been carved into the psyches of everyone who has called Chattanooga home.

The city of Chattanooga has been blessed by being known for its mountains and rivers rather than its skyline or cityscape, as most other cities are known. The city does have its architectural landmarks, though. The aquarium is especially well known, as is the Dome building and the old mansion at Bluff View. Perhaps the most notable, though, for its grand design and the rumors that swirl around it, is the Patten Towers at the corner of Eleventh Street and Georgia Avenue.

The Patten Towers was once known as the Hotel Patten. In the weeks before its opening, the Hotel Patten was grandly heralded as being the finest hotel in the country. It was among the finest in the world, some said, and on the morning of April 1, 1908, hundreds of local citizens lined the streets awaiting the hotel's noonday grand opening. For weeks, the local papers had been printing daily stories detailing the new construction's progress, building a sense of anticipation and local pride the city had never before experienced. The Civil War had become history, the South was rebuilding and Chattanooga was on the verge of becoming the greatest city in the region. Everyone came, from governors and mayors to local farmers who left their work in the fields and brought their families to town to see the new "skyscraper." The Dynamo of Dixie was drawing crowds from hundreds of miles away, and it was guessed that the opening of this

Vintage image of the Hotel Patten. *Library of Congress.*

new hotel would double the population of the city. Chattanooga already had the steamboats and barges on the river, the rail yards and depots and the steel factories. Now everyone had come out and filled the dusty streets to stare up in awe at the grandest architectural accomplishment in the land.

The Hotel Patten was indeed a sight to behold. It stood eleven stories tall, an unimaginable height in its day, and had a face of terra cotta, pressed brick and white marble. The building stood proudly against Chattanooga's April sky. Bands played in the streets outside, and women laughed out loud. Children ran in circles, and men in their best clothes stood on Chattanooga's old dirt streets and smoked and talked, their chests a little larger as they stood in the shadow of the marvelous building.

When those first visitors finally passed through the hotel's front doors, they entered a lobby with ceilings twenty-eight feet high, with crystal chandeliers scattering the early light. The floor was marble tile, the walls were a beautiful scagliola onyx and great columns of Georgia marble supported the ceiling.

Surrounding the lobby on three sides was a richly furnished balcony. The plush and elegant furniture there was made from mahogany and was specifically designed by the hotel's architect. A house orchestra performed on this balcony, sending strains of sweet music floating and echoing through the hotel's halls.

The East Restaurant, or main café, was pronounced by all to be the most elegant and comfortable dining room in this or any other country. Plate glass windows touched gold leaf ceilings and flooded the dining room with the cool spring light. The floors were English red tile and the walls quartered oak. On the menu were Russian caviar and English sole, prepared by a French executive chef, and an Italian baker and pastry chef had left one of the largest hotels in New York City to join the staff at the Hotel Patten. All the help employed in the kitchen were white, it was proudly declared, and there was not a novice among them.

Chattanooga could not have been more pleased. The great clothing designers from New York often came down to display the newest fashions. Parties were hosted in the grand ballrooms. High society ladies and well-kept gentlemen fancied one another there.

One of the hotel's lesser-known accommodations was an underground tunnel that provided privacy for the famous and elite. The great hotel played host to governors, presidents and celebrities from all walks of national life. Jimmy Hoffa kept a room there when he was standing trial in 1964 at the nearby federal courthouse. John Kennedy visited the hotel, as did countless Hollywood and musical celebrities who passed by train through the South. The Hotel Patten was, by all accounts, a place fit for kings.

But it was not to last. Forty years after the hotel opened its doors, just after the Second World War, President Eisenhower began his interstate system. Everything was soon to change. Automobile design and construction had come a long way from the days of the old Model T. Cars had become serious, fast machines designed for far more travel than the occasional trip over bumpy roads into town. They were meant to travel. With them came the freight hauling trucks that would soon give even the powerful railroads a run for their money.

When those World War II soldiers came back home to the States, they found their waiting wives and a surplus of young girls ready and willing. It didn't take long for the nation's "Greatest Generation" to conceive and soon give birth to the baby boomers. The United States' population exploded in the 1950s, and the drought of the Great Depression was over. The war was over. The economy was booming, and there was a lot of hope in the land. The boys and girls had been separated for a long time, and there were fast cars to be had and new highways to drive them on. The good times began rolling. But back to Chattanooga.

The nearest interstate highway in the 1960s was Interstate 75, which connected Atlanta to Knoxville. Interstate 75 bypassed Chattanooga. It may have been assumed that because Chattanooga was still a major hub of railroad traffic, the city had no need of a major interstate highway passing through its limits. But by the 1960s, this was no longer assumed, and work on Interstate 24 had begun.

The mammoth task of installing Interstate 24 was talked about for years. It required "moving the river," the engineers said, and despite all odds, the awesome feat was eventually accomplished. Interstate 24 branched off Interstate 75 and connected the city of Chattanooga to Nashville and to Interstate 40 beyond. Interstate 40 travels all the way to the West Coast, and Chattanooga's people and industries became connected to the rest of the nation.

The new cars and Eisenhower's interstate system—the new way people and freight were carried across the country—put an effective end to passenger rail travel. Much of Chattanooga was dependent on the old rail commerce, and the Hotel Patten was especially concerned. People no longer paid for extended nights in hotel rooms. Cheap motels began popping up right off every freeway exit. They didn't offer elegant, full-service experiences with five-star dinners and tuxedoed waiters in the evenings. They offered cheap beds for the night and maybe a biscuit in the morning. People had places to be—not to mention the big truck drivers who began hauling scheduled freight over the interstates rather than waiting for it to be loaded onto freight cars pulled by train engines. The luxuriant, pampering hotels, of which the Hotel Patten was one of the grandest, became a thing of the past. The hotel was eventually sold to a man from Miami, a big hotel and motel man who planned to rebuild the place into apartments for the elderly. In 1977, a week before Christmas, newspaper writer Bill Casteel wrote an article for the *Chattanooga Times* describing the Hotel Patten's final days. It was a poignant description of a Chattanooga that was slipping sadly away to history:

> *An off-duty bartender sits at the bar, chatting softly with a couple of the few remaining regulars of past days.*

The lighting is subdued. Candle flames flicker nervously as they fight to stay alive at the bottom of their holders.

It is mortuary quiet until the on-duty bartender's shrill voice demands that "someone play the juke box."

The wake is under way for the Lamplighter Restaurant and Lounge in the Hotel Patten.

The strains of Elvis Presley's "Blue Christmas" filter through the lounge, beyond the swinging doors and into the spacious lobby outside.

A group of long-time residents of the hotel huddle in little groups and talk about their years at the Patten. Some of them have tears in their eyes as they discuss the imminent demise of what has become home to them.

Susie Neligan has become an institution there, making the Patten her home for 40 years, 37 of which were spent in the same room. She still remembers her first night there.

"I went down the next morning and asked the gentleman at the desk—I don't remember his name, but he had been a football star at UC—how long I could stay here. He said 'until doomsday.'

"Well, this is doomsday."

Miss Neligan and about 20 other elderly people were given notice Thursday that they must find new homes. The Patten is closing down, to be renovated and reopened as an apartment complex for the elderly.

Although these and other occupants of the hotel have until Jan. 15 to relocate, the elderly will have to find new quarters as soon as possible. The restaurant where most of the oldtimers have had their meals for decades is shutting down Monday night, a prelude to the hotel closing.

Walking the streets to find an eating place won't be easy for folks like Miss Neligan, whose eyesight is failing and who walks with a cane.

"I don't know where I'll go," a near-sobbing Miss Neligan sighed. There are others in the same predicament, including Miss Sarah Raht, the sweetheart of the hundreds of railroaders who have "roomed" at the Patten during their stopovers there.

Mrs. Raht plans to live with her daughter until she can find a permanent place downtown.

"It's home here," she said, in much happier tones than some of the other hotel residents. "We have had a grand crowd here for many years. The railroad men have been so nice to me. I just love them all. I'm going to miss them and they're going to miss me too."

A Southern Railway employee who had been chatting with Mrs. Raht smiled in agreement.

With the departure of the railroaders and others who knew eviction was just a matter of time, business in both the restaurant and lounge has slumped.

For all practical purposes the Hotel Patten and adjacent lounge and restaurant will be interred Monday night. Some of the occupants will likely hold out until their 30 days' notice is up in January. But without the eating and drinking facilities, the hotel will become much like a ghost town.

No longer will one be able to witness such bizarre and diverse sights as a Pentecostal revival, where souls were being saved and afflictions cured, on one floor, and walk down a flight of stairs to where hangovers were being made.

A jukebox that was forever too loud will go silent, as will the pinball machines which made their way onto the scene during the lounge's last days.

Live entertainment, some of which bordered on big time, more of which was amateurishly awful, will be a thing of the past.

The closing of the Lamplighter and Patten comes at a time when many are already melancholy. Little wonder, then, that employees and patrons alike talk in hushed tones when the shutdown is discussed. Small wonder, too, that coin after coin is dropped into the jukebox to play what has become this establishment's swan song, "Blue Christmas."

For the 18 employees of the restaurant and lounge, the holiday spirit has been dampened by the word that Monday night marks the finish to their present jobs.

Al Sweeney, owner of Patten's Lamplighter Restaurant and lounge, said his employees will be given severance pay and a Christmas bonus to take some of the sting out of their loss of jobs.

Sweeney is planning one final bash for his lounge regulars and others Tuesday night.

The curtain closer, Sweeney said, will be held to offer "one final look at the place before it closes."

Kind of like viewing the body before the burial.

By January 1978, it was all over. An auction house had come in and put price tags on everything inside the grand hotel. The beds, doorknobs, desks and lighting fixtures were all being bought and carried out the front doors. Even the telephones and water faucets were sold. Everything that could be moved was torn down and sold to the highest bidder. Ms. Helen Exum wrote an article for the *News Free Press* expressing her sadness over the dismantling of the proud old landmark and remembering her younger days when the hotel was Chattanooga's pinnacle of elegant society:

We would get dressed up in our best clothes, put on white gloves and wear a hat, and walk up the steps where the doorman would open the door into the lobby. Miss Fan would greet each person with a hug and a kiss, make little exclamations of delight with a compliment or two. Then we would go into the beautiful dining room and sit at round tables, I think. She usually chose chicken salad in the summer, chicken a la king in the winter. After dessert came finger bowls. Being a lady and going to the Patten was a wonderful way of life, now very nostalgic.

One month later, on January 15, 1977, what was once the Hotel Patten closed its doors forever. Soon thereafter, the old hotel reopened and eventually became what it is today: the Patten Towers, a federally subsidized project-based facility for the elderly and disabled operating under a Section 8 contract with the U.S. Department of Housing and Urban Development. And ever since the old building made this change, bizarre stories have circulated about what goes on behind those old walls. Strangely, most of the stories revolve around fire trucks that arrive screaming at the building's front steps nearly every day. According to Chattanooga Fire Department records, fire trucks respond to calls from the Patten Towers about three hundred times every year.

The nearest neighbor of the Patten Towers is the Pickle Barrel, a pub on Market Street whose back door faces the building. I was sitting at a table by the window eating lunch there one afternoon, watching the people from the Towers hang out on the sidewalks outside and mulling over the odd fate of the place—how something that was once the pride of the entire city could have fallen to such absurd depths. It was just a brick building, but the strange tales that revolve around it have reached nearly legendary proportions. I asked my waitress in the pub what she knew about the old hotel. She laughed. "They sell their crazy meds on the sidewalk out here," she claimed. "And when they get their monthly checks, they come in here and eat hamburgers. That's where the taxpayers' dollars are going," she added as she walked away. "Hamburgers at the Pickle Barrel."

Another employee taking a break at a table beside me offered a second story. She claimed to be standing near the back door one night and watched a puddle of liquid sneak in from under the door. When she opened the door, she found a man standing there urinating. She and a cook chased the man away, she said, and she laughed when she told me how the man held his side and started yelling, "I only have one kidney! I only have one kidney!" She believed the man to be a resident of the Patten Towers.

The two girls went on to work, and an old friend of mine came in for lunch and sat nearby. I asked him if he knew anything about the Patten Towers. He laughed, too, and offered an explanation for the frequent fire calls. "They all get their checks on the first of the month and start burning their mattresses," he claimed. I told him that sounded ridiculous, but he said, "No. Residents of the Patten Towers set their mattresses on fire when they get their checks. It's common knowledge." He couldn't explain why they would do such a thing; he only knew that it was so.

I didn't believe anything I'd just been told, especially the bit about the burning mattresses. But as absurd as my old friend's explanation sounded, there had to be some reason the fire trucks roared up to the old building with such strange frequency.

Hoping that curiosity wouldn't be the death of me, I set out down Market Street one morning to see what there was to learn. I passed the Pickle Barrel and walked up the old Hotel Patten steps. The front door was locked, and a security guard at a desk behind the door was unwilling to let me in. He just looked at me as I pulled on the door and shook his head no. I went back down the steps, wondering what to do next just as another man came up the steps beside me. I stopped him and asked if he lived there. He said he did. I told him I was interested in the history of the Pattern Towers and wanted to write a story about the old hotel.

"I'm the one you need to talk to, then," he said. "Come over here a minute." He hurried back down the steps, around the corner and out of sight of the front door. He looked at me with a curious smile and asked if I was Robert T. Nash, a local radio personality. I said I wasn't and told him my name. His name was Robert Earl.

"Yeah, you don't really sound like him. I've called in and talked to Robert Nash a few times. He hangs up on me too much. But look here, you got any credentials so I'll know who you are? I'm not trying to be funny, but you know…" I explained that I was nobody important and had nothing more than a driver's license.

"Well, you seem all right. I usually get a feeling about people. I can tell. What is it you want to write about?" I told him I was interested in the building's history and what it had become. "Oh yeah, man. I lived here for five years," Robert told me. "This place goes way back. It's a real nice place. Presidents stayed here. Actresses and movie stars. What was that gangster's name? Jimmy Hoffa. Man, it's a nice place."

I told him I'd like to see inside, and he said he'd be glad to take me. I followed Robert up to the front door. He swiped a card and pulled the door open. "Tell the guard up here you're going to 302," he said, then vanished around the corner. Once inside, the security guard took looked me over pretty hard but took my presence in stride. I signed my name on a visitor's log with the guard and was a bit surprised that he not only asked for my driver's license but also said that he'd have to keep it until I left.

At the elevator around the corner, Robert reappeared and told me we'd stop and let me look around on the second floor. I recognized that second floor as the ballroom from pictures in books and old newspapers, but the elegance was gone. There was no longer a balcony looking down onto the first floor. The second floor was now full of folding tables and chairs, and drab government-issue tile had replaced the Georgia marble. A few people roamed around, but there was certainly no ball going on, celebrity-filled or otherwise. Robert explained that a local Seventh-Day Adventist Church had for years served Thanksgiving and Christmas dinners to the residents on this second floor but for some unknown reason had not come that year.

A laundry room was around the corner. Washers and dryers lined the walls there, and the building's gold ceilings and marble columns were gone. Plain fluorescent lighting had replaced the chandeliers. I didn't hear any orchestra, and no one offered me caviar or martinis. But I didn't smell any fires burning.

I followed Robert up a flight of stairs to his apartment. "Here we are," he said. "Home sweet home." Home was an efficiency apartment overlooking the city. It was well kept and quiet. Pictures of his family hung on the walls, and a blanket was thrown over the back of his couch. Recent newspapers and local periodicals were stacked neatly under an end table. Of particular interest to me was a bookshelf in the living room filled from end to end with books on offbeat spirituality. There were no beer bottles piled high or drunks sleeping it off in corners. I sat on his couch and looked out the window onto the city below.

"You know, this is a nice place," he said. "It's not big or fancy, but I got everything I need." Robert had a gallon of sweet tea in his refrigerator, and he shared it with me. We talked about the city mayor's office being right around the corner. Robert said that he'd been over to talk to the mayor a time or two—he was a real nice guy, he said. There had been rumors of the Patten Towers being emptied of its tenants once again and renovated. Some said there were people who wanted to turn the building into high-dollar condominiums. Robert doubted it would ever happen, and to prove his point, he pulled out a VHS tape from a collection of them he had and slid it into an old VCR. It was a recording he'd made of a roundtable discussion between city leaders from a show that appears on a local public broadcasting station at some unwatchable hour of the morning. The mayor participated, and on the videotape he repeated what Robert had said.

Time to go came, and on the way back down the elevator, an older woman stepped on. Robert obviously knew her. He asked the woman how a recent surgery had gone. The woman shook her head and smiled, saying it went as well as surgeries go. Hearing this, I realized that I never asked Robert how he qualified to live there. I didn't ask him then, either—just thanked him and left once we reached the first floor again.

A few days later, I called Robert to ask him about all the bizarre stories that are told on Chattanooga's streets. I told him what everybody said and asked him why the Patten Towers had the reputation it had.

"Let me tell you something about Chattanooga, man," he said. "Chattanooga's a negative damn town. Everybody's always got something to say. Everybody wants to say something, but they usually ain't about nothing. You know what I mean? Everybody's got to have somewhere to sleep. And ain't nobody perfect. But it ain't nothing like what you read about. I mean, you been in there. You know."

"Let me tell you something, though," Robert went on. "I don't mean to change the subject. This whole city is got a bad vibe. I took a class one time that showed you how to use your mind in different ways—how to use parts of your mind that you don't normally use. I can feel stuff. I'm wrong sometimes, but usually I'm right. I mean, this is a negative place. You know UTC used to be a prison with gallows, man. I know people who've walked around there and won't go back. They used to kill people up there. I'm not saying it's ghosts, but it's something. It's like that all over this town. This whole town's like that."

I set up a time to meet with Robert Earl again. I was supposed to meet him for lunch a week or so later. I was sitting in the Pickle Barrel as fire trucks once again howled toward the front door of the Patten Towers. The residents slowly ambled outside. Some of them struck up conversations with the firemen who were there. None of them seemed to be in any hurry. I waited awhile, but Robert didn't show up. I called him on the phone. He said he wasn't going to be able to make it that day due to the fire alarm. The call had come from the floor he lived on. He said he wasn't going to stand out in the cold waiting for the fire trucks to leave and had caught a ride to a friend's house. I asked him what he knew about the fire call and why the trucks were there again that day. He said most of the fire calls were from people burning things on their stoves while cooking. He knew the woman living in the apartment who set this smoke alarm off and said she shouldn't have been cooking anyway.

"She can't even stand up," he said.

The Strange Death of John Caree

The Henry Wiltse manuscript that has been preserved by the Chattanooga public library holds a wealth of information that will not be found in the standard regional history books. The stories of Orchard Knob and the first turkey theft, retold in this book, are but two. There is the dry history in the old manuscript as well—the economics and sundry politics of a city's life—but Wiltse had the habit of recording things that are out of the realm of normal interests. He recorded strange happenings and mysterious, unexplainable occurrences that Chattanooga has mostly forgotten. There were the odd behaviors of Chattanooga's earliest leaders, such as former congressman William Crutchfield spouting his powers as a "water witch" and explaining his theory of the "divining rod"—he publicly challenged any who discredited his claims to come test his water-finding gifts. Wiltse wrote about "the discovery of a regular trade in human bodies which were being shipped express as fish" out of Chattanooga. He wrote down many such tales. The history of Chattanooga has not been a succession of good ideas implemented by smart mayors. There is a quiet, whispered history that most would prefer to not see. The historian Wiltse noted many such odd happenings in the manuscript he left behind. Among them were:

"Spectral lights" that were seen on the river several times at different points, which caused interest, speculation and no little awe.

The disappearance of Katy Kaveny, and the opening of C.C. Whitney's grave. The bones were removed and effort was made to burn them.

An epidemic of hiccoughs that prevailed to some extent.

In the places known as Black Hills and Blue Pond it was asserted that human blood was found in chunks.

Around a maple tree, in an alley between Magazine and Prospect Streets there occurred a shower every day about two o'clock in the afternoon, for *a period of ten days. Just around this particular Maple tree, and not elsewhere. This was an early October occurrence.*

An interesting mystery was "a mysterious and luxurious little red houseboat" which turned out to be a pirate craft.

A leading sensation, especially among a certain class of colored folk, was the ghost of Buddy Wooten in action at the county jail, where Buddy had been hanged.

Rosa House, negress, and Jim Roberts were found dead on East Ninth Street, their throats slashed from ear to ear.

Voodoo and witch doctor practices. It was said graves had been robbed to get fingers, etc. to wrap in feathers.

Chinese residents here celebrated their picnic for the dead at Forest Hills Cemetery, in March 1890.

This was the "Kissing bug" year, too.

There are those who delight in such tales, and small businesses have been set up that thrive on people's fascination with the odd and macabre. Chattanooga Ghost Tours will take visitors to the city on a strange and haunting tour; its guides tell their visitors a few of the more commonly accepted tales of the weird. They will show them the Read House, where in room 311 a Union soldier murdered a young prostitute long ago. They'll take them to see the

The Crutchfield grave today. *Author's collection.*

tunnels and caverns of the lost city beneath Chattanooga's streets. Their tours go to a lot of strange places. One tale recorded by Henry Wiltse that those tours do not tell, however, and one that is known to very few, is that of the strange death of John Caree.

John Caree was a black man. In 1878, John Caree, like so many other Chattanoogans that year, came down with the dreaded yellow fever. He was taken from the saloon where he worked on Market Street and sequestered at the pest house, where those infected with the virus were being quarantined. It was there at the pest house, at six o'clock one morning, that John Caree died. At nine o'clock that same morning, John Caree was taken to the Citizens Cemetery across the street from the college and dumped in the black earth without ceremony.

Twenty-nine years later, on January 18, 1907, John Caree was called by Chattanooga attorney Jim Easley to the city courthouse. Poor John Caree was then led to the witness stand and placed under oath. He swore to tell the truth, so help him God. The first truth he told was that he had no knowledge of the case then being tried and had no idea why he was being made to testify in a court case he knew absolutely nothing about. He added for emphasis that everyone in the courtroom knew that he had no knowledge of the current trial, the judge and lawyers included. He then asked why he was being bothered. The courtroom authorities smiled at him and told him that they were the ones who asked the questions.

Jim Easley then began questioning him. The following account of the death of John Caree was given by John Caree himself while under oath and in regulation court testimony:

Attorney Jim Easley: How old are you, John?

John Caree: I don't know how old I am.

Attorney: Did you live here in 1878?

John Caree: Is that what you brought me here to tell? I guess I did live here then.

Attorney: Did you have Yellow Fever?

John Caree: They said I did and I guess I did.

Attorney: How long was you dead?

John Caree: I don't know.

Attorney: Where did they take you when you took the fever?

John Caree: To the pest house, just like any other man.

Attorney: Who took you to the pest house?

John Caree: Bill Johnson.

Attorney: Did you die there?

John Caree: Of course I didn't die. I just went off in a trance just like any other man would go off in a trance.

Attorney: Did you wake up again?

John Caree: Yes, I woke up just like any other man would wake when they was trying to get in my grave.

Attorney: Did they put you in a coffin?

John Caree: Of course they put me in a coffin just like any other man.

Attorney: And buried you?

John Caree: Well, they put me down in a hole, I reckon I was buried.

Attorney: What did you have on your finger?

John Caree: A ring. It belonged to a woman and after I was buried they came to get it. They came about 10 o'clock that night, I reckon.

Attorney: Did they get the ring?

John Caree: Well, when I heard them pounding on the box it sort o' roused me and when they begun pulling on my finger to get that there ring I just set right up. Them fellows broke and run.

Attorney: How did you get out of the grave?

John Caree: Well, there wasn't nobody to help me out and I just clumb out like any other man.

Attorney: What did you do then?

John Caree: I don't know what I done that night. The first time I came to myself I was on Market Street with nothing on but my undershirt and slips.

Attorney: Where did you go?

John Caree: To Pettibone's where I had worked. It was a saloon on Market Street down by the river.

There is no record of what transpired once John Caree reached the saloon down by the river. What happened at the saloon that night can only be guessed. This writer feels entirely certain, though, that John Caree asked for a stiff whiskey, and most likely received one. He may have had a number of them. Later, presumably, he slept.

The rumor of John Caree's death and resurrection had floated around Chattanooga since the days of the yellow fever. John Caree had apparently been reluctant to tell the tale, so the city authorities conspired to drag the truth from him in open court. They succeeded in doing so, and the speculation was ended. They heard it from the man himself. After hearing his version of the events, attorney Jim Easley and the court released John Caree. It is further

The Citizens Cemetery today. *Author's collection.*

assumed that he mumbled and cursed a little, left the courthouse and went home to live out the rest of his days, hopefully in peace.

John Caree may have eventually died again. If so, and perhaps at his own request, it's never been told where he was buried the second time. He may be in some unmarked grave in the old Citizens Cemetery again, or he may be beneath the earth in a patch of woods at the foot of Lookout Mountain somewhere.

Or maybe John Caree did the Lazarus trick and rose once again. Maybe he is not beneath some patch of Chattanooga earth. Maybe he crawled out of his grave once more and is shuffling through this weird life still. He could have floated down the river to New Orleans and found a place in an Anne Rice novel. He might have stuck around Chattanooga—maybe he's a high school janitor now or a barber or a preacher. He could be a taxicab or school bus driver. He could even be sitting in the drunk tank at the jail in Chattanooga right now, getting angry about the prospect of having to talk to some Chattanooga lawyer yet again.

Who knows?

LEGENDS OF NICKAJACK CAVE

Chattanooga is hollow beneath the ground. There are the manholes that lead to tunnels that were once sidewalks and to dark passages that meander off into the sides of what were once street-level storefronts. There are the old rooms and the dark, hollow places behind long-locked doors beneath the city streets. Lost somewhere in those dark passageways is the subtle secret that is the spirit of Chattanooga.

There are caves in the mountains and along the river, and there are spirits of the past in those dark places, too. There are a lot of these caves. There is the much-loved Ruby Falls, that wonderful destination cave. There are the Raccoon Mountain caverns. Along a trail on the side of Lookout Mountain, there is another cave (now with a steel door bolted across the entrance) that is said to have natural wonders far exceeding those of Ruby Falls. A little farther down the river, there is yet another nearly forgotten cave, with which we are now concerned.

It is said that in 1780, an Indian war party, while fighting white settlers at Stone's River near Nashville, captured a black freeman named Jack Civil. Jack was an accomplished blacksmith and was well known for his smithy skills. The Indians did not know the blacksmith's art, and for this reason, Jack Civil's life was spared. After the battle, Jack was taken back east with the war band and brought to a cave near Ross's Landing known by the natives as Te-calla-see. There his skills proved extremely useful to the Indians' militant efforts. In time, he became trusted by the tribe and was eventually held in high esteem.

Outside settlers learned of the dark-skinned blacksmith who lived among the hostile Indian tribe. The white men began referring to Te-calla-see as Nigger Jack's Cave. Outside Indian tribes, too, began referring to the mysterious and dangerous cavern above the river by this name. Due to their native pronunciation and broken English, the dark cavern eventually became known by the name we call it today: Nickajack Cave.

The environment outside Nickajack Cave was dangerous and violent in those old days. That black cave mouth opened out of the side of the mountain and looked down on a stretch of the Tennessee River then known as the Narrows. The water was turbulent and dangerous then, and on either side of the river, the mountains rose up, in some places as sheer rock walls. Nickajack Cave was found in these environs—a dark, terrible hole in a land that was alive and cruel. Even the fertile valleys surrounding the cave were uninhabited by the forest natives. Indian scouts and hunters avoided the place. When forced to pass the Narrows and the mysterious cave, the Indians would glide silently and swiftly by, their eyes watching the shadows behind the trees and the blackness of the cave mouth. Nickajack Cave was a place for devils.

The recorded history of Nickajack Cave begins before there was the city of Chattanooga. It begins when there was only Ross's Landing on the river's edge. It begins with what the Cherokee Indians considered the theft of their land.

In the middle of the eighteenth century, bearded white settlers began leaving the northern states and traveling southward, seeking the abundance they had heard was growing among the rivers and valleys of the wild southern lands. There were mountains there that no white man had ever seen—lands unnamed that were free for the taking. There was hope in that land. This was a new world, untamed and free, and a thousand years of European wisdom and bravado was going to create a new society here the likes of which the world had never known.

But the wild land they hoped to civilize belonged to another people. The Cherokee Indians had inhabited the lands in the Chattanooga valley for

Site of John Ross's Landing today.
Author's collection.

thousands of years. To them, the earth beneath them was as sacred as the white man's God up in the sky. These natives did not consider their land free for the taking, and skirmishes ensued between the natives and the settlers. Men on both sides were slain, and homes were burned. Women and small children screamed as knives rose above them. The settlers faced enemies who considered their very souls tied to the land. They were not going to let it go as easily as was hoped.

The new government in the North, having founded itself on liberty and moral reasoning, felt it necessary to become involved. The nation had recently declared its independence, famously stating in 1776, "We hold these truths to be self-evident, that all men are created equal, that they are endowed by their Creator with certain unalienable Rights, that among these are Life, Liberty and the Pursuit of Happiness." In light of this, it was decided that a diplomatic approach to the natives would be necessary.

So, promises were made to the Indians. Treaties were written. It was decided that the land should be purchased fairly, and if the native population didn't want to sell the land, then common morality deemed that they should at least share some of it. At times, the land was simply traded for blankets, rope and cheap rum. For £2,000 sterling and six wagonloads of useful goods, a man named Richard Henderson purchased 20 million acres from the Cherokee Indians. This deal, known as the Henderson Purchase, bought almost all of the state of Kentucky and a large portion of middle Tennessee.

The money and the wagonloads of guns, rope and rum were given only to a certain few of the tribal elders and old chiefs. The traditional hierarchy of the native tribes deemed this proper, and it greatly suited the wishes of the white purchasers. The few chiefs and tribal elders who received the goods were satisfied with the deal. The rest of the Cherokee nation, unlearned in the ways of European commerce and fair trade, soon started feeling like they had been stolen from.

A young Cherokee warrior, Dragging Canoe, had long opposed any land treaties with the white men and warned the settlers after the Henderson Purchase that they would soon be walking over a "dark and bloody ground." Dragging Canoe wanted his people to rise up against the invading Europeans, but the elder Cherokee leaders were opposed to war with the white men. The bearded Europeans were beginning to fight among themselves, anyway—in 1776, the American Revolution began, and the British were coming. Let it all be, they said. They won't last. But Dragging Canoe would not. This young warrior stood up before his people after the Cherokee chiefs and elders signed yet another such deal with the white men and gave this now famous and prophetic speech:

Whole Indian Nations have melted away like snowballs in the sun before the white man's advance. They leave scarcely a name of our people except those wrongly recorded by their destroyers. Where are the Delewares? They have been reduced to a mere shadow of their former greatness. We had hoped that the white men would not be willing to travel beyond the mountains. Now that hope is gone. They have passed the mountains, and have settled upon Cherokee land. They wish to have that usurpation sanctioned by treaty. When that is gained, the same encroaching spirit will lead them upon other land of the Cherokees. New cessions will be asked. Finally the whole country, which the Cherokees and their fathers have so long occupied, will be demanded, and the remnant of The Real People, once so great and formidable, will be compelled to seek refuge in some distant wilderness. There they will be permitted to stay only a short while, until they again behold the advancing banners of the same greedy host. Not being able to point out any further retreat for the miserable Cherokee, the extinction of the whole race will be proclaimed. Should we not therefore run all risks, and incur all consequences, rather than submit to further loss of our country? Such treaties may be all right for men who are too old to hunt or fight. As for me, I have my young warriors about me. We will hold our land.

Dragging Canoe gathered together a militant band of other young warriors and attacked a white settlement near the Holston River. For this, a reward was offered for the young warrior's death, and he was expelled from the Cherokee nation. Dragging Canoe responded by saying that the peaceful Cherokee were nothing more than "Virginians and Rogues." Rather than give in to the treaties and constant westward expansion as the older men had, Dragging Canoe left his home, his father and his land near Knoxville, Tennessee. With a small band of young warriors, he headed south.

The exiled band traveled by raft and canoe down the Tennessee River and eventually took up residence in Te-calla-see, the cave we now call Nickajack. The dreaded site was chosen for the new settlements because Dragging Canoe felt it would be advantageous, being near the dark cave and near a path where hunting parties of the Creek Indians crossed the river. In a short time, many of the Indians who had been forced to flee their homes along Chickamauga Creek because of new white settlements took up their quarters with the exiled Cherokees. Dragging Canoe declared asylum for his people there. Furthermore, Dragging Canoe declared that any native who would devote himself to resisting the advance of the white men would be made welcome. He soon established the Indian towns of Running Water, Lookout, Long Island and Crow in the valleys surrounding the cave.

On dark nights and in the fire-lit depths of the cave, Dragging Canoe began handing out knives to his new young warriors. Hidden in the darkness of Nickajack Cave, the exiled Indians danced their war dances and shouted for their gods to grant them strength and bravery, as they were soon to begin attacking any white settlement on Indian land.

Thus was born the fierce band of Indians that later became known as the Chickamaugas. Led by Dragging Canoe, they became the most feared warring tribe in the southeastern states, their war cry being, "We are not yet conquered."

From his stronghold at Nickajack Cave, Dragging Canoe soon became the greatest warrior and defender of their land the Cherokee nation had ever born. The Chickamaugas waged a vicious war on the white settlers. The Chickamauga tribe grew in strength and numbers under the leadership of Dragging Canoe, and no raft or fleet of settlers passed the river outside Nickajack Cave. Controlling the waterway at the Narrows as he did, Dragging Canoe effectively stopped the settlement of western Tennessee in his lifetime. For more than a decade, Dragging Canoe and the Chickamauga warriors slaughtered every person who crossed this land unwelcomed. The river ran red, and the walls of Nickajack Cave became covered with the scalps of white men.

The land was lawless in those days. The Tennessee valley was then a part of the American frontier—a terrible place where a man's life depended on his aptitude for self-reliance and primal savagery. The violence and the savage landscape with which all men were faced can scarcely be imagined today. Despite the federal government's early attempts to establish order in the furthest reaches of the New World, the only true law was the territorial animal law to which all the men involved were bound—the natives and the new settlers. Dragging Canoe fought with the amoral viciousness of the worst of them, and in his lifetime, he succeeded in holding his land. Because of his fierce determination and his stronghold at Nickajack Cave, he effectively halted the European settlement of western Tennessee in his lifetime.

In March 1792, Dragging Canoe's brother ferociously attacked the John Collingsworth family along the Cumberland River near Nashville. Mr. Collingsworth, his wife and daughter were all brutally killed. Dragging Canoe had stayed behind to meet with the Muskogee and Choctaw tribes, eventually convincing them to join forces with his Chickamauga tribe in the war against the white settlers. His brother returned to Nickajack and told him of the successful attack against John Collingsworth. Dragging Canoe demanded a scalp dance to celebrate the killings and his recently made alliances. The fires, dancing and shouting raged all through the night. Dragging Canoe celebrated the occasion madly, singing war songs and dancing the ecstatic Eagle Dance through the cold night. While he danced, Dragging Canoe ground the scalp

Artistic rendering
of an Indian
dance near the
Tennessee River.
Author's collection.

of a white man between his teeth. Dragging Canoe danced until he collapsed. He died the following morning from the frenzy of that night's dancing.

It didn't take long for the federal commanders to learn of the death of Dragging Canoe. A successor was soon appointed to lead the Chickamaugas, but with the death of their true leader, the white men knew that the Chickamauga tribe had lost its ferocity.

In 1794, the federal government launched what has become known as the Nickajack Expedition. Under the command of U.S. Army major James Ore, 550 mounted infantrymen were sent from Nashville to destroy the Chickamauga settlements. Among those infantrymen was a young private who had intimate knowledge of the Chickamauga settlements and the terrain around Nickajack Cave. He would later be known as President Andrew Jackson and would be responsible for sending the eastern Indians on what the Cherokee later called the Trail of Tears.

On the night of May 12, these infantrymen men crossed the river about four miles below Nickajack Cave. They slept at the edge of the river that night. The following morning, the soldiers took the natives by complete surprise. At Nickajack, the soldiers found two scalps that had recently been taken and all the others hanging on the walls as trophies. The men then began the slaughter. No Indian was spared—women and dead children were scattered over the ground outside Nickajack Cave. This infantry burned the villages and destroyed everything resembling the native civilization at Nickajack, leaving only their smoldering fires and the Chickamaugas' sacred land saturated with blood.

There was nothing remaining of the warrior Dragging Canoe. His people were slaughtered, their homes burned and their ground muddy with blood. The towns Dragging Canoe established were destroyed. Yet despite the loss of his cause, Dragging Canoe died faithful to the Chickamauga war cry—he was never conquered.

AND LET GOD DO WHAT HE DOES WITH PEOPLE LIKE ME

In 1967, another man staggered into Nickajack Cave. He was a man who had made his name rambling around playing a flat-top box and singing about trains and guns and prisons. He sang about loose women, drunken Indians and lazy dogs. He sang about shoeshine boys and floods. Chain gangs and men swinging from gallows. Railroads and rivers. He sang about waking up in a Chattanooga jail one morning and said he taught the weeping willow how to cry.

He ran with Elvis Presley through the early days of rock-and-roll, singing, "I don't care if I do—die—do—die—do" from Memphis to New Orleans.

He went to sing for the convicts in California's Folsom Prison one day. He carried his flat-top box up the backstage steps and looked out over a room full of murderers, robbers and thieves. He wore a black suit. He saddled up his guitar the right way, walked on out to the microphone and said, "Hello, I'm Johnny Cash."

But in 1967, the music men in Nashville were saying that the Man in Black was through. He stood six-foot-two, weighed 150 pounds and had long been strung out on cocaine, pills and booze. Johnny Cash was sick. He had been in and out of hospitals and jails for years and had canceled countless concerts because he was too wasted to stand on a stage and sing. By the beginning of October that year, he was on the edge of death. He had been awake for days and hadn't eaten anything other than amphetamines by the handful. He was whiskey drunk and strung out, and he knew that his career, as well as his life, was near its end.

He left his home in Hendersonville, Tennessee, one day that October and drove east for an hour or so. He parked his old Jeep on the side of the road and then staggered through the thorns and brush down to the mouth of Nickajack Cave. He walked into the blackness of that cave until he could walk no more. He then went to his hands and knees and crawled until he couldn't crawl anymore. Like a sick animal, he was looking for somewhere to die.

Johnny Cash was born into a fundamentalist Christian family. His early life was dominated by hard work, family, church and gospel radio. The preachers on the radio, in between the gospel songs, said that Jesus died for the fundamentalists' sins and that the symbolism around which the faith is built carves itself into the souls of all its believers. It is preached that every man is born sinful, guilty and bound for Hell. Unless a man accepts the bloody sacrifice at Golgotha—the "Place of the Skull" where Jesus was nailed to a wooden cross and sacrificed—then one is bound for Hell. One must believe that Jesus rose from the dead and be washed in his blood. Once this blood-cleansing has been made, one's name will be written in the Lamb's Book of Life—on the final Day of Judgment, one's name must be found in this book or be damned to burn in the eternal fires. Every man is born guilty of every sin, the fundamentalists say, and forgiveness for this overwhelming guilt must be begged for. Johnny Cash was taught to believe these fire-and-brimstone preachers, as were most young farm boys in his day. The reward for accepting the inherited guilt and begging forgiveness for it would be everlasting life in a heavenly city with streets of gold. The punishment for denying the guilt would be eternity in a lake of fire.

But there was a consuming darkness in Johnny Cash, a darkness that was wholly intertwined with that sense of Christian guilt but was never explained by those preachers on the old gospel radio stations. This darkness came from somewhere deeper than Christianity. It was a brutality and a strange affinity for the sinful and "bad men" of the world. Johnny told of it in his songs—most famously in "Folsom Prison Blues," when he sang about shooting a man in Reno, not in a feud over a woman or in a dusty street duel, but "just to watch him die." The dark brutality found in "Folsom Prison Blues" doesn't waste time justifying itself or making sad excuses. It's not revenge or jealousy—it's death for death's sake. It was the Man in Black's murder ballad side.

There's another such ballad in which a woman named Delia is murdered. The killer in that ballad tied Delia to a chair. He shot her once—it didn't kill her, he said, and he found it hard to watch her suffer. So he shot her again, and "with the second shot she died." Johnny Cash wrote many songs such as these.

But there is a catch, and there was always this catch in those murder ballads of his. At the end of the songs, Johnny Cash always tells of the guilt the killer later felt. Every time he thinks about that dead man in Reno, he hangs his head and cries. When the law finally catches up with Delia's killer, he's suffering the jailhouse consequences and pleading for the jailor to come help him, crying that he can't sleep because all around his jailhouse bed he hears the "patter of Delia's feet." The guilt is always there, and that sense of guilt is what made the seemingly senseless brutality understandable to all of us.

Nobody believes that Johnny Cash actually murdered a man just to watch him die. He didn't do what he said was done to Delia. He was a master songwriter, and these murder ballads are just finely crafted songs. But there is something of the real Johnny Cash in those songs. The truth that's in those dark ballads, which came from the bottom of Johnny Cash's soul and what elevates his songwriting so far above all others, is the remorse his murderers always felt.

Johnny Cash had lived on the road for years, traveling and singing his songs about killers and floods, jailhouses and whores. He ate pills to keep running and became "leather and bones," he said, and there was nothing left of him. He had no idea who he was anymore. He thought that in the black depths of Nickajack Cave, he could put an end to his life and nobody would ever find his wasted body. Only God would know where he was, and he was ready to let God put him "wherever He puts people like me," as he said later in his autobiography. That heavy guilt had wholly overcome him, and he felt there was no redemption for himself anymore. He had no control—death was the only way to make the guilt of what he had become stop. He wanted to be swallowed in the blackness of the Nickajack Cave and of the peaceful blackness of death. He had laid himself down to die.

Then something happened. He later said:

> I didn't believe it at first. I felt something very powerful, a sensation of utter peace, clarity and sobriety. I couldn't understand it. How, after being awake for so long and driving my body so hard and taking so many pills—dozens of them, scores, even hundreds—could I possibly feel all right? The feeling persisted though, and then my mind started focusing on God. There in Nickajack Cave I became conscious of a very clear, simple idea: I was not in charge of my destiny. I was not in charge of my own death. I was going to die at God's time, not mine.

The Man in Black then raised his head. He started to move. He had no idea how to get back out of the cave, but he crawled in whatever direction he could find, feeling before himself with his hands. He soon felt a breath of wind on his back. He turned around and followed that wind until he saw a light.

When he came out of the blackness, he found June Carter standing at the mouth of Nickajack Cave. She had a basket of food and gave him something to drink. She held his arm, and Johnny told her that God had saved him in that cave. She drove him back home, and Johnny told her that he wasn't going back to what he was before. He had been unable to forgive himself for what he'd become, but there in the blackness of Nickajack Cave, he realized that God would forgive him.

The traditional symbolism of the cave tells us that those dark spaces beneath the earth are where spiritual death takes place prior to rebirth. Passing through a cave represents a change of state, or a reentry into the womb, and reemergence represents that rebirth or spiritual enlightenment. The story of Johnny Cash at Nickajack Cave fits this mythic symbolism perfectly. He entered Nickajack Cave as the Man in Black—strung out, road-worn and with a deep darkness consuming his soul. He entered that cave as a guilty man, but the Man in Black reemerged forgiven and a Man of God.

But he still had songs to sing. In his last years, Johnny Cash recorded some old gospel songs. One of those songs seems to tell the tale of what happened to him in the dark depths of Nickajack Cave. As he sang this song, there was a new truth in his old voice. It was not the shaky guilt that was there when he sang about tying Delia down or watching that man in Reno die. It was a religious conviction. Johnny didn't write the song. It's an old spiritual that tells of the righteous brutality of God rather than of the brutality and guilt that Johnny often sang about—that age-old evil guilt that is born into all men:

> *Well my Goodness Gracious! Let me tell you the news!*
> *My head's been wet with the midnight dew!*
> *I been down on bended knee*
> *TALK-in' to the Man from GAL-i-lee*
> *He spoke to me with a voice so sweet*
> *I thought I heard the shuffle of angel's feet*
> *He called my name and my heart stood still*
> *When he said, "John, go do my will!"*
> *Go and tell that long-tongued liar, go and tell that midnight rider,*
> *Tell the rambler, the gambler, the back biter,*
> *Tell 'em that God's gonna cut 'em down.*
> *Tell 'em that God's gonna*
> *cut 'em*
> *down.*

But the Man in Black is gone now. Dragging Canoe is gone. Johnny Cash doesn't play the flat-top box anymore, and the blood that once saturated the ground at Nickajack Cave has been washed away. Trees have grown up outside Nickajack Cave, where dead women and children once lay.

A dam was built in 1967, and Nickajack Cave was flooded—no one is allowed to go inside. All the Indians are gone, and Johnny Cash was one of the last men in there. There's a fence around the cave's mouth now. The place is now home only to a colony of gray bats that fly out when the sun goes down. When darkness falls and the gray bats fly out, the moon rises over the river and moonlight floats on the water. It's quiet outside the cave at night. There are the shadows of the mountains, the moonlit river and a soft wind.

Nothing else is there.

AFTERWORD

With heavy heart, I have been forced to omit a number of tales from this collection—a lack of space and, in some cases, simple prudence have left a stack of stories lying in a dark closet. Anyone so interested could resurrect these stories themselves. It is a fascinating glimpse into the picture album of Chattanooga's past and serves to remind us all that as much as times have changed, we as a people have not. The pathos, crimes, general goodness and sometimes general idiocy that colored the lives of those living centuries ago is no different than what is found in the lives we live today.

Among that pile of newspaper clippings and discarded pages are tales such as the tragicomedy of Poor Loffland. He was as inconsequential as the rest of us, too. He was a man such as any other man of his day. His tale is one every man has lived through, though—every man who has loved and devoted himself to one of the fairer sex knows Poor Loffland's story. But that wife of Poor Loffland—that pretty young girl who promised to stand beside him for better and for worse, through sickness and in health, through good times and through bad until death did they part—how did that pretty young wife respond to Poor Loffland's wedded devotion? She shot him through the head—and in the back of the head, no less. She shot him in the back of the head while he was riding ahead of her on a horse, so he never saw it coming. A gentleman's graciousness would declare that she shot him thus from sympathy, hoping to inflict a quick death and to so charitably spare him any emotional pain. This would be because women are gathered to be the fairer and softer and more loving of the species. But upon learning Poor Loffland's tale, common sense declares that she shot him in the back of the head and not between his unbelieving eyes because she was scared.

Cowardly, even, but she was a woman, and women cannot be thought of in such ways. Only men can be cowards. Women are simply afraid.

But the cruelty of it all—she was his wife. His very own wife. And the most bizarre aspect of his tale is that he did not die. He chased his wanton and unfaithful wife all through the city and surrounding towns for days with a bloody bullet hole in his head. He eventually captured her, only to have his faithful pleas refused by her once more.

There is the tale of the Taylor boys—of the hotheaded murder that one of the boys committed on a Chattanooga riverboat. This man Taylor was arrested for the crime, only to be brazenly recaptured by his outlaw brothers while shackled in a train heading for his trial in Knoxville. The brazen exploits, killings and subsequent hangings of the Taylor brothers were legendary in their day. The tale has now been buried in the filing cabinets of the Chattanooga library and in the graves of all those who lived it.

There are the tales of lynchings on the Walnut Street Bridge and of clandestine Ku Klux Klan doings—one of the Klan's secret meeting places was recently discovered in an upstairs room of an old downtown Chattanooga building. There are stories falling out of the windows of that place. There are stranger stories of mayors and congressman bragging over the quality of their fruit trees and of their prowess at witching water from the ground, while the Ku Klux Klan was meeting in that upstairs room. There are many more such tales, all now forgotten.

Contrary to popular historical opinion, not every historical tale involves large movements of soldiers or the political deeds of sundry politicians. There are tales that are seemingly ordinary and unimportant but somehow offer peculiar insights into the character of a people. Mr. Weathers and his silly thieving admission, as well as the more serious or foreboding tales of other unknown and unimportant characters from Chattanooga's past, let today's citizens know their true forbears. The stories of these people—these dead nobodies, some would say—are our stories. The past deeds of war generals and mayors, statesmen and big businessmen, play most miniscule parts in defining who a people are. Some may care about the actions of Mayor Carlile in the time of yellow fever or of the state governor's reaction to the Chattanooga floods, but most do not. Most would be much more interested in the charity of those such as Hattie Ackerman and Harry Savage. And why? Those concerned with the mayors and governors would ask why the actions of some poor, unknown little schoolteacher or some kindhearted thug should be more important to today's citizens than those of the great leaders of the past. The answer to this is very simple: we are not descendants of the leaders of the past. Their failures and accomplishments are not our own—they belong to whoever follows in their well-shoed footsteps. The average man today has Harry Savage and Hattie Ackerman to call their own and to be proud of. Let today's mayors, judges and governors have those such as themselves. They are of no real consequence to anyone other than future mayors and judges, anyway. They are not who Chattanooga is.

There was a book written one time—a book that is surely sitting in a bookstore or on Chattanooga library shelves somewhere. It's a book that is very well known to aficionados of American literature, which is to say that most people have not read it. It is called *Spoon River Anthology*, and it tells the story of a small fictional town by singing the epitaphs written on the graves of the town cemetery. It is a small masterpiece, a reckoning of the life of common people written as honestly as writing was allowed to be in its day. Remember the tale of Andy Williams and his old Orchard Knob? Of the historian Wiltse asking him to recall the senseless bloody days of the Civil War, but Andy wanted instead to remember riding his sled down the side of the old hill and the whippoorwills at night? The beginning of this old piece of literature recalls something of that:

> *...They brought them dead sons from the war,*
> *And daughters whom life had crushed,*
> *And their children fatherless, crying—*
> *All, all are sleeping, sleeping, sleeping on the hill.*

> *Where is Old Fiddler Jones*
> *Who played with life all his ninety years,*
> *Braving the sleet with bared breast,*
> *Drinking, rioting, thinking neither of wife nor kin,*
> *Nor gold, nor love, nor heaven?*
> *Lo! he babbles of the fish-frys of long ago,*
> *Of the horse-races of long ago at Clary's Grove,*
> *Of what Abe Lincoln said*
> *One time at Springfield.*

Old Fiddler Jones knows our true history. He would be my kind of guy—drunk and raising hell, thinking neither of wife nor money nor God—only hanging around fish fries and playing his fiddle for sandwiches and booze. Fiddler Jones knows something of the truth. Lots of books have told us over and over again all the things that Abe Lincoln said, but Old Fiddler Jones knows what we all felt when Honest Abe said it, as well as the idle banter at the fish fries and those old horse races: our history is in what was said there, not written on some war memorial plaque on the side of the road somewhere. What Abe Lincoln said at Springfield can't matter nearly as much as how the people of Springfield felt about it. Old Fiddler Jones is who could tell us what we felt. He could also tell us what prayers those fatherless children might have said before they themselves grew old and went to sleep on the hill, hoping to again see in the afterlife the fathers they lost in Abe Lincoln's war. Old Fiddler Jones, fiddling drunk though he was, paid close attention to those children's prayers and to other things of such small consequence. The presidents have so many bigger things to worry about—speeches and proclamations, fellow politicians and potential assassins and so forth. President Lincoln, just as our politicians today, knew nothing of what was said at the horse races at Clary's Grove or on the cold mornings little girls spent laying flowers on their daddy's graves.

But it borders on treason to bad-mouth Honest Abe. Everyone loves Abe Lincoln, as do I, but it should be accepted that he is not as important to us as some have made out. He's not who we are. He is not where we come from. It is true that he was a great statesman who made very great decisions, but his decisions were made for us and, sadly, in spite of some of us. He was a politician the same as our politicians today, and his decisions, deeds and proclamations tell us that he was one of the greatest American politicians, but he was nothing more. He is not who we are—his story tells us nothing of ourselves. Again, dead presidents are for future presidents just as dead mayors are for forthcoming mayors—they are not for us. There may have been times in our youths when we saw something of ourselves in the histories and portraits of those called great in our country's political past, but things such as our first jobs and those first years out of college quickly steered us away from the White House and back toward our own families and our own hometowns pretty quickly, and with a newfound understanding of what that singer John Mellencamp sang one time: "Hey boy, you gonna be President! But just like everything else all them old crazy dreams just kind of came and went." But we do have those pink houses he sang about, and we do have our pasts and our pride—they are all our own and that is who we are.

I'm no fiddle player and I'm certainly not Fiddler Jones, but here in your hands is my version of what Old Fiddler Jones offered to the world—small stories of our past and the land around us. To learn who we once were, we must listen to the old drunk fiddlers and to Johnny Cash, to John Caree and the ghost of Buddy Wooten. We must listen to those workmen who shoveled river mud from the city streets after the floods, to Andy Williams and his skunk-sprayed girlfriend and to all the old black men locked up in prisons like that young boy Haywood Patterson. To understand the spirit of Chattanooga, we must listen to the symphony of all those lives as inconsequential as our own. We must tell our sons to look past themselves—past us, even—and to remember the stories of all those now-forgotten people who were once as bright and alive as we all are.

ABOUT THE AUTHOR

Cody Maxwell is a contributing writer for *The Pulse*, an alternative newsweekly. He is currently at work on a second historical book about the Chickamauga Indian warrior Dragging Canoe's dealings with pirates on early American rivers.